Understanding AuDHD

Fourth edition

Psychology that helps you

Lee Hopkins

°138

Published by degrees138, Adelaide, South Australia

Formatted with Vellum

For Hương,
who pays attention.

And for everyone who spent decades
believing the problem was them.
It wasn't.

'The trouble with having an open mind, of course,
is that people will insist on coming along
and trying to put things in it.'

— Terry Pratchett

'I may not have gone where I intended to go,
but I think I have ended up
where I needed to be.'

— Douglas Adams

Author's note

This book was co-written with Claude, an AI made by Anthropic. I am telling you this in the first pages rather than burying it in an acknowledgements section because transparency about how a book was made seems more respectful to the reader than hoping they don't notice, and because the question of whether AI-assisted writing is 'real' writing is, in my view, the wrong question asked by the wrong people for the wrong reasons.

Here is how it worked. Every argument, claim, personal story, clinical observation, and editorial decision in this book is mine. I directed the structure, chose the sources, determined the voice, and made every call about what stayed and what got cut. Claude drafted prose from my instructions, suggested connections I hadn't considered, tracked references with a reliability my ADHD brain cannot match, and produced output at a speed that would have taken me, working alone, approximately three years rather than three months. The ideas are mine. The research verification is collaborative. The sentences were produced by an AI and edited, reshaped, and inhabited by a human until they sounded like me rather than like a machine pretending to be me, which is a distinction any reader with a functioning ear can detect and most critics with a functioning agenda will ignore.

The question I find more interesting than 'is this real writing?' is: what happens to a neurodivergent author whose executive function makes sustained long-form writing physiologically expensive when they gain access to a tool that handles the physiological expense while preserving the intellectual and creative control?

The answer, in my case, is that they write a 50,000-word book in the time it would previously have taken to write one chapter, and the book is better than it would have been without the collaboration, because the human's energy goes into thinking rather than into the mechanical production of sentences, and thinking is what the human was always good at.

If this troubles you, I understand. The relationship between human creativity and machine capability is genuinely unsettled, and anyone who claims to have resolved it is selling something.

What I can tell you is that every word in this book passed through a human mind that has lived the experience it describes, and that the mind in question would rather be honest about its tools than perform a fiction of solitary genius that was never true for any writer and is less true now than ever.

The fan wobbles. The coffee is mine. The AI helped with the paragraph.

Preface to the fourth edition

The third edition of this book was a guide. The fourth edition is an argument with practical tools.

The difference matters. The third edition said: here is what AuDHD is, here is how it presents, here is how to manage daily life with it. That book did its job. It helped people. I still hear from readers who say it was the first thing that made their experience legible.

I am proud of it in the specific, limited way you can be proud of something that was as good as you could make it at the time and is no longer as good as you can make it now.

Three things changed between editions. The research moved. I moved. And the world surrounding the book moved in ways that changed what the book could afford to assume.

The research: since the third edition, the field has begun recognising AuDHD as a distinct neurological profile rather than a comorbidity, which is the argument Chapter 1 makes and the foundation on which the rest of the book stands.

The allostatic load evidence connecting neurodivergence to measurable physical health consequences has matured from scattered findings to a coherent picture that Chapter 3 documents and that nobody is talking about with the urgency it deserves.

The dementia research has arrived. The MCAS connection has been published.

Emma Craddock's 2026 study has given us the first phenomenological account of women's lived experience of AuDHD. The research base for this edition is substantially different from the one that supported the third, and the clinical implications are more serious.

I moved: from Adelaide, Australia to Đà Lạt, Vietnam. From a disability pension below the poverty line to a comfortable expatriate life funded by the same pension in a cheaper economy. From decades of systemic depression to something that looks, cautiously and without triumphalism, like contentment. Same brain. Different environment.

The evidence for this book's central argument, that AuDHD outcomes are shaped more by environment than by neurology, is sitting in a café writing the preface.

I published eight books between editions, each of which informs specific chapters and is cross-referenced throughout: *Misdiagnosed, It's the circumstances, The Body Remembers the Fire, Harder than it should be, You're Not Imagining It, The Convenient Monster, The Augmented Psychologist,* and *The Collapse of Knowledge.* This edition draws on the constellation. It does not repeat it.

The world moved: a Substack ecosystem of neurodivergent writers, clinicians, and academics has emerged as arguably the most important site of AuDHD knowledge production in 2026, operating outside institutional structures, funded by readers rather than grants, and producing scholarship at a speed and depth the academy cannot match.

Chapter 11 documents this ecosystem in detail. The writers it features, Bridgette Hamstead, Lindsey Mack, the Autistic Standpoint Theory author, and others, have directly informed the arguments in multiple chapters.

The structural shift from the third edition is the addition of an argumentative spine. The practical material remains: executive function tools, sensory management, relationship navigation, healthcare advocacy, educational and employment strategies.

But running through the practical chapters is a sustained argument that 'living well with AuDHD' is not primarily an individual project. It is a systemic one.

The systems—economic, educational, healthcare, social—that AuDHD people navigate daily are designed for a different brain, and the cost of navigating them is not just psychological but physiological, measurable in allostatic load scores and life expectancy data and the particular quality of exhaustion that accumulates across a lifetime of performing someone you are not.

The book's new chapters reflect this shift. Chapter 3, on allostatic load and the dementia evidence, is the controversial one. Chapter 14, on the systems that shape neurodivergent outcomes, is the argumentative one. Together they transform the book from a guide that helps individuals cope to a case that the coping should not be necessary in the first place.

The voice has not changed. I still write as if we are at a kitchen table and nobody needs impressing. The humour is still load-bearing. The Australian bullshit detector is still operational. The cosmic perspective, that we are mammals with credit cards trying to run nervous systems that predate spreadsheets, still provides the frame.

What has changed is that the person at the kitchen table has moved countries, survived a collapse, rebuilt a life, and has less patience for advice that points the arrow inward when the evidence points it outward.

If you read the third edition and found it useful, this edition will deepen the understanding. If this is your first encounter with the book, it is designed to stand alone.

And if you are reading this in a waiting room, about to be assessed for something you have suspected for years, the only thing I want you to know before the first chapter is this: whatever they find, you were never the problem. The distance between you and the world was the problem, and this book is about understanding that distance, measuring it, and figuring out what to do about it now that you can see it clearly.

Đà Lạt, Vietnam

March 2026

Chapter 1

AuDHD is not a comorbidity

The friend who changed my life did it over coffee, which is appropriate because most of the important things in my life have happened within arm's reach of caffeine.

Gaye is a psychologist who has worked with veterans for years, helping us navigate the distance between service life and the civilian world, which can be a chasm dressed up as a career transition.

She is also one of the people who has seen me at my absolute worst and my bouncy best, which is a wider range than most friendships are asked to accommodate and which she has accommodated with the particular grace of someone who understands that both versions are the same person operating under different loads.

She asked me, with the studied innocence of someone who already knew the answer, whether I'd ever considered that I might be neuro-divergent. She let me discover it for myself, which is what the best friends do. It is also what the best clinicians do, though the overlap between those two categories is rarer than the profession would like to admit.

What followed was an informal assessment. Not a formal one. My disability pension would not cover the considerable cost of a comprehensive diagnostic evaluation, which in Australia runs into the thousands and is means-tested by a system that apparently believes the people least able to afford assessment are the ones who need it least.

But there was a second reason the assessment remained informal, and it is the reason this chapter exists: a formal assessment would almost certainly have produced the wrong answer.

The diagnostic tools available to any clinician conducting a formal AuDHD evaluation are designed to identify two separate conditions. Autism assessment tools look for autistic traits. ADHD assessment tools look for ADHD traits. The training, the instruments, the scoring frameworks, the report templates, all of them are built on the assumption that you are measuring two things that happen to coexist in the same person.

It would be extremely unlikely that any diagnostician, however skilled, would be able to avoid separating the autism and ADHD sides of my brain, because the system they work within was designed to separate them.

The co-occurrence framing is not just a theoretical position. It is baked into the tools. And the tools, applied to me, would have produced a report describing two conditions sharing a nervous system, like flatmates who'd ended up in the same house by administrative accident and were now arguing about the thermostat, the grocery list, and whether silence constituted a valid form of communication.

Gaye, who knew me as a whole person rather than as a collection of symptoms to be sorted into diagnostic categories, could see something the formal tools would have missed: that my brain was doing something particular, coherent, and spectacularly poorly understood my entire life. Not two things. One thing, with a logic the diagnostic system had never been designed to recognise.

Something about that framing, the wholeness of it, bothered me for months afterward. Not because it was wrong. Because it was the first thing that had been right about my brain in four decades of psychiatric attention, a sentence that should probably concern someone at the Royal Australian and New Zealand College of Psychiatrists but almost certainly won't.

What kept nagging was the realisation that a formal assessment, the one I couldn't afford, might have been less accurate than the informal one I received from an educated friend who knew me, because the formal system would have produced exactly the two-conditions framing that my lived experience contradicted.

I wrote about the moment that recognition landed, what it felt like to discover at sixty-six that the question everyone had been asking about my brain for forty years was the wrong question, in the opening chapter of *Misdiagnosed.* I called it 'The question that changes everything,' because it does.

When you stop asking 'What's wrong with this person?' and start asking, 'What if the diagnostic framework is wrong about this person?' the entire landscape shifts. This chapter picks up where that one left off.

I've spent the fourteen months since that conversation with Gaye reading the research, talking to other AuDHD adults, working clinically with neurodivergent clients, and paying closer attention to my own brain than I have since my twenties, when I was mostly using it to make poor decisions about romantic partners and career choices, sometimes simultaneously.

What I've found is that the co-occurrence framing, whilst technically defensible, may be the wrong lens entirely. And that the wrong lens, applied for long enough, distorts everything downstream: the research, the clinical practice, the support structures, and most importantly, the way AuDHD people understand their own experience.

This chapter makes a different argument. AuDHD may not be autism plus ADHD. It may be its own thing.

HOW WE GOT THE QUESTION WRONG

To understand why the co-occurrence framing dominates, you need the history. And the history, like most histories of psychiatric classification, is a story about confident people being wrong in interesting ways for a surprisingly long time.

The Diagnostic and Statistical Manual of Mental Disorders—the DSM—is the reference book most clinicians in the English-speaking world use to classify mental health and neurodevelopmental conditions. It occupies a curious position in medicine: simultaneously indispensable and routinely embarrassing, like a GPS that gets you to the right suburb but consistently parks you in the wrong driveway.

Until 2013, the DSM contained an explicit prohibition: you could not diagnose autism and ADHD in the same person. The DSM-IV stated that ADHD could not be diagnosed if the symptoms were better explained by an autism spectrum disorder. One or the other. Pick a lane.

This wasn't based on evidence that the conditions couldn't coexist. It was based on the diagnostic philosophy of the time, which preferred clean categories over messy reality. Autism went in one box. ADHD went in another. The boxes were assumed to be separate rooms in the same building, and nobody thought to check whether the wall between them was load-bearing or decorative.

Clinicians knew this was a problem. They'd been seeing children who clearly displayed features of both conditions for years.

A child whose social communication difficulties pointed toward autism but whose impulsivity and inattention screamed ADHD had to be filed under one label or the other—a process with all the diagnostic rigour of sorting laundry by guessing what colour it was before it faded.

The decision often came down to which symptoms were loudest in the assessment room on that particular day.

Autistic traits that manifested quietly—the sensory sensitivities, the internal rigidity, the grinding exhaustion of navigating unwritten social rules—could be overshadowed by the more visible ADHD presentation: the fidgeting, the interrupting, the spectacular inability to sit still during a forty-five-minute assessment designed by someone who apparently believed that sitting still for forty-five minutes was a reasonable thing to ask of any child, let alone a neurodivergent one.

The DSM-5, published in 2013, removed the exclusion criterion. For the first time, clinicians could officially diagnose both conditions in the same person. The American Psychiatric Association acknowledged, with the quiet understatement that characterises institutions admitting they've been wrong for decades, that the previous approach had been 'overly restrictive.'

Which is one way of putting it. Another way would be: we spent thirty years telling people their lived experience was diagnostically impossible, and we'd like to move on without discussing that too carefully.

The removal was genuine progress. But it came with a framing that embedded itself in everything that followed: two conditions, now permitted to coexist. Two diagnoses on the same report. Two sets of criteria, two bodies of research, two treatment literatures, applied to one person and stapled together.

I wonder whether that framing has been asking the wrong question ever since.

WHAT THE NUMBERS ACTUALLY TELL US

The co-occurrence statistics are striking enough to make you put your coffee down, which, given the attention span of the average AuDHD reader, is saying something. A meta-analysis of 63 studies by Rong and colleagues found that the pooled current prevalence of

ADHD among autistic people was 38.5%, with a lifetime prevalence of 40.2% (Rong et al., 2021). Roughly four in ten autistic people also meet criteria for ADHD. That's not a statistical footnote. That's nearly half the population.

In Australia, autism affects approximately 1 in 40 people. ADHD affects around 6 to 10% of children and adolescents and 2 to 6% of adults. When you factor in the Rong co-occurrence rates, the population of people living with both conditions is far larger than the diagnostic infrastructure in most countries was built to identify or support. We're not talking about a rare overlap. We're talking about a substantial minority of all neurodivergent people, navigating a system designed on the assumption that they don't exist.

But here's where the statistics start telling a more interesting story than the co-occurrence framing allows.

A 2025 real-world study of 2.3 million insurance members found that people with both autism and ADHD had comorbidity patterns that were synergistically different from either condition alone (Thomas Craig et al., 2025). Not additive. Synergistic. The health profile of AuDHD was not 'autism health problems plus ADHD health problems.' It was something else—a distinct pattern that neither condition's literature predicted.

When two conditions produce outcomes that can't be explained by adding their individual effects together, the standard scientific response is to ask whether you're looking at a single phenomenon rather than two separate ones.

In chemistry, when two elements combine to produce something with entirely different properties, we call that a compound, not a mixture. Sodium is a metal that explodes in water. Chlorine is a gas that will kill you. Combine them and you get table salt, which does neither of those things and goes quite well on chips.

I wonder whether AuDHD might be a compound rather than a mixture. The research is beginning to suggest it might be.

WHEN TWO BECOMES SOMETHING ELSE

The lived experience of AuDHD, when you listen to the people inside it rather than reading about them in clinical abstracts, does not sound like two conditions taking turns. It sounds like a single system with its own particular, occasionally baffling, logic.

Consider the internal experience that most AuDHD adults describe: a simultaneous craving for routine and novelty. Not alternating. Simultaneous. The autistic architecture wants predictability, structure, sameness. The ADHD architecture wants stimulation, variety, the next interesting thing.

In the co-occurrence model, these are opposing forces pulling in different directions. In lived experience, they feel like a single river with crosscurrents—not two rivers flowing in opposite directions through the same landscape.

The Vanderbilt University Frist Center for Autism and Innovation has been exploring this complementary dynamic. Their work suggests that the autistic need for structure can actually help manage ADHD distractibility, providing scaffolding that pure ADHD brains lack. And ADHD's impulsivity can help autistic people break out of rigid routines that might otherwise calcify into paralysis.

The traits are not fighting each other. They're negotiating, constantly, in ways that produce something neither would produce alone.

I recognise this negotiation in my own experience with the weary familiarity of someone who has been living inside it for sixty-seven years without a manual.

My autistic capacity for deep, sustained focus on topics that engage me is extraordinary. I can disappear into research for days without sleep and surface knowing more about allostatic load than most people would consider reasonable or, frankly, attractive at dinner parties.

My ADHD makes that focus gloriously unreliable in any context that doesn't trigger my interest system—which includes most administrative tasks, most social obligations, and approximately 94% of what the neurotypical world considers 'normal adult responsibilities.'

But the two traits don't feel like separate forces. They feel like a single attention system operating by rules that nobody wrote a manual for, because nobody recognised it as a single system long enough to study it properly.

Late in 2025, a research team led by Priya Rajasethupathy at Rockefeller University published findings in *Nature Neuroscience* that may explain why (Rajasethupathy et al., 2025).

They identified a gene called Homer1 that influences attention by shaping how quiet or noisy the brain is at rest. Mice with reduced levels of specific Homer1 variants showed calmer baseline brain activity and performed better on tasks requiring focus.

Homer1 has been independently linked to both ADHD and autism—not as a gene for one condition that happens to affect the other, but as a gene involved in the neural processes both conditions share: sensory processing, attention regulation, and the filtering of relevant from irrelevant information.

If attention improves by reducing neural noise rather than increasing stimulation, then the traditional ADHD model—which frames the condition as a deficit requiring chemical amplification—may be addressing only half the mechanism.

And if the same genetic architecture influences both autistic sensory processing and ADHD attention regulation, the case for treating these as separate conditions sharing a body becomes harder to sustain.

One gene study in mice does not overturn decades of clinical categorisation, and anyone who tells you otherwise is selling something. But the Homer1 findings join a growing body of evidence suggesting that the neural substrates of autism and ADHD overlap in ways that are structural, not incidental.

If that's true, then AuDHD isn't two conditions in one brain. It's one neurological profile that our diagnostic system, built on the assumption of separate categories, has been splitting in half.

WHAT THE PEOPLE INSIDE IT SAY

The most compelling evidence that AuDHD is its own thing comes not from genetics labs but from the people living it. And in 2026, the first formal phenomenological study of that lived experience was finally published—which tells you everything you need to know about the speed at which academia responds to questions communities have been answering for years.

Emma Craddock, writing in the journal *Health*, conducted interpretative phenomenological analysis of interviews with women diagnosed with both autism and ADHD in adulthood (Craddock, 2026). Her conceptualisation was striking: she framed AuDHD as a 'residual diagnostic category,' a condition not formally represented in diagnostic systems, existing in the space between two recognised diagnoses that don't quite capture what the person is experiencing.

Which is a polite academic way of saying: the filing system doesn't have a folder for you, so we've been jamming you into two folders at once and wondering why the edges don't line up.

What her participants described was not two conditions coexisting. They described a fluid, dynamic experience in which autistic and ADHD traits interacted to produce something that felt, from the inside, like a single way of being in the world.

The descriptions were revealing in their inconsistency: one participant called them 'two separate parts of my brain,' another described them as 'two sides of the same coin,' a third drew the distinction that 'autism is a part of me, ADHD is an add-on.'

These descriptions don't agree with each other. But they share something important: they're all improvisations. People trying to describe a unified experience using the only language the diagnostic system has given them, which is the language of two separate conditions.

When the available vocabulary doesn't match the lived reality, people improvise. And the improvisations, collected together, start to reveal the shape of what the vocabulary is missing.

Bridgette Hamstead, whose Substack has become one of the most important platforms for neurodiversity scholarship, argued in a March 2026 series that AuDHD research is undergoing a 'critical turn,' shifting from studying AuDHD as a subtype of one condition or the other toward recognising it as requiring its own phenomenology, its own research frameworks, and its own clinical approaches.

The field is beginning to treat AuDHD as a distinct entity. The diagnostic systems have not caught up. They rarely do. Diagnostic systems move at the speed of committees, and committees move at the speed of people who have never personally experienced the thing they're classifying.

WHAT CHANGES WHEN YOU CHANGE THE LENS

If AuDHD is an emergent profile rather than a co-occurrence, several things follow that matter practically, not just theoretically.

Assessment needs to change. Most existing diagnostic tools were developed for single conditions. Autism assessments look for autistic traits. ADHD assessments look for ADHD traits. Neither is designed to capture the interaction between them—the ways one set of traits modifies, masks, or amplifies the other.

An autistic person's rigid adherence to routine can suppress visible ADHD hyperactivity, making the ADHD invisible to an assessor looking for fidgeting. An ADHD person's social impulsivity can mask autistic social difficulties, making the autism invisible to an assessor looking for withdrawal. When the conditions interact, both can hide in plain sight—a neat trick if you're a magician and a catastrophe if you're a patient.

My AuDHD was identified informally at sixty-six, by a friend who knew me well enough to see the whole picture rather than the fragments a formal assessment would have produced. For the preceding forty years, the psychiatric system had been treating me for bipolar disorder, depression, and anxiety—a cascading sequence of misdiagnoses I documented in full in *Misdiagnosed*, for anyone who wants to understand what happens when the wrong question is applied to the right brain for four decades.

I responded poorly to every medication they tried, which they interpreted as treatment resistance rather than wrong diagnosis. Nobody asked whether the attention problems, the sensory sensitivities, the social exhaustion, and the relentless internal restlessness might be a single neurological profile rather than a collection of psychiatric symptoms. The question wasn't available, because the diagnostic framework didn't contain it.

I received treatment for conditions I didn't have, and no treatment for the condition I did, for longer than many of my readers have been alive.

Treatment approaches need rethinking. AuDHD medication management is notoriously complex because stimulant medications that help ADHD attention can increase autistic sensory sensitivity and anxiety, while strategies that help autistic overwhelm—reducing stimulation, increasing predictability—can worsen ADHD understimulation and boredom.

Treating the conditions as separate problems creates an impossible clinical game of whack-a-mole, where addressing one set of symptoms worsens the other. The mole, in this metaphor, is your entire nervous system, and the mallet is being wielded by someone who thinks there are two moles.

Treating AuDHD as a single profile with its own internal logic suggests a different approach: finding the interventions that work with the whole system rather than targeting half of it at a time.

And perhaps most importantly, self-understanding changes. The co-occurrence model tells AuDHD people they have two problems. The emergence model tells them they have one brain that works differently.

The emotional distance between those framings is enormous. I spent forty years believing I was broken in multiple ways simultaneously, which is exhausting in the way that only compound self-blame can be. Understanding that I have a single neurological architecture—coherent but different from the majority—didn't eliminate the challenges. But it reframed them from evidence of compound failure to evidence of operating an unusual system without a manual.

That reframe shouldn't matter as much as it does. But when you've spent decades believing you're failing at being human in several different ways at once, discovering that you're actually doing one unusual thing consistently is, in a way that's genuinely difficult to convey to someone who hasn't lived it, profoundly liberating.

THE MISCONCEPTIONS THAT PERSIST

Several misconceptions continue to complicate public understanding and clinical practice. They're worth naming because you will encounter them, probably from well-meaning professionals who learned their neurodevelopmental psychiatry before the field caught up with the people it was studying.

The most persistent is the idea that autism and ADHD are incompatible because autism involves restricted interests and ADHD involves distractibility. This misunderstands both conditions with impressive efficiency.

Autistic restricted interests are not about inability to be distracted;

they're about the intensity and depth of focus when the interest system is engaged.

ADHD distractibility is not about inability to focus; it's about unreliable deployment of focus across contexts. An AuDHD person can hyperfocus on their special interest for eight hours and be unable to sustain attention on a tax return for eight minutes, and this is not a contradiction. It's the system working exactly as its architecture predicts. The architecture just wasn't designed for tax returns, which may tell us more about tax returns than about the architecture.

The masking misconception is particularly damaging. If someone can appear neurotypical in social situations, the reasoning goes, they can't have significant neurodevelopmental differences.

This is rather like arguing that because someone can run a marathon on a broken ankle, the ankle must be fine.

A woman who has learned to make appropriate eye contact, laugh at the right moments, and perform social ease while internally tracking seventeen unwritten rules and managing sensory overload from the restaurant's lighting is not evidence that she's fine. She's evidence that masking is an extraordinary and unsustainable cognitive achievement that the diagnostic system routinely mistakes for health.

The timing misconception also causes real harm. Many people receive one diagnosis in childhood—usually ADHD if the hyperactivity is visible—and don't receive recognition of their autistic traits until adulthood, sometimes decades later. This creates the impression that the person 'developed' autism in midlife, which is neurologically nonsensical.

What happened is that the scaffolding—the routines, the relationships, the coping mechanisms keeping the autistic traits below clinical visibility—eventually collapsed under accumulated strain. The autism was always there. The diagnostic system couldn't see it until the supports gave way, at which point it was startled to discover something that had been present since birth. Diagnostic systems are frequently startled. It is one of their least endearing qualities.

A DIFFERENT STARTING POINT

The question is no longer whether autism and ADHD can co-occur. The DSM settled that in 2013, though it took the diagnostic establishment roughly three decades longer than it took the people living it. The question now is whether 'co-occurrence' is the right frame for what is actually happening when both conditions are present.

Whether the research that treats AuDHD as a subtype of autism, or a variant of ADHD, or a statistical overlap between two independent conditions, is missing something that the people living it have been trying to articulate for years.

The evidence is accumulating. The genetics suggest shared neural mechanisms. The epidemiology shows synergistic rather than additive health patterns. The phenomenology describes a unified experience that diagnostic language struggles to capture.

The community has been using the term AuDHD precisely because neither condition's label, applied alone or in combination, describes what it actually feels like from the inside.

This book takes that evidence seriously. Throughout the chapters that follow, AuDHD will be treated not as two conditions sharing a body but as a distinct neurological profile with its own internal logic, its own strengths, its own vulnerabilities, and its own requirements for understanding and support. The interaction is the thing itself, not a complication arising from two separate things.

The next chapter explores what that profile actually does in daily life—which is where the science meets the kitchen on a Tuesday morning when you've lost your keys for the third time whilst simultaneously remembering, in extraordinary detail, a conversation about quantum physics you had six years ago.

AuDHD is a particular kind of brain. Understanding it on its own terms is, I'd argue, the most interesting scientific and human question the neurodevelopmental field isn't quite asking yet.

Let's ask it.

REFERENCES

American Psychiatric Association. (2013). *Diagnostic and statistical manual of mental disorders* (5th ed.). American Psychiatric Publishing.

Craddock, E. (2026). Navigating residual diagnostic categories: The lived experiences of women diagnosed with autism and ADHD in adulthood. *Health, 30*(2), 235–257. https://doi.org/10.1177/13634593251336163

Hopkins, L. (2026). *Misdiagnosed: What happens when the psychiatric system gets the question wrong for forty years*. degrees138.

Rajasethupathy, P., et al. (2025). Genetic mapping identifies Homer1 as a developmental modifier of attention. *Nature Neuroscience*. https://doi.org/10.1038/s41593-025-02155-2

Rong, Y., Yang, C.-J., Jin, Y., & Wang, Y. (2021). Prevalence of attention-deficit/hyperactivity disorder in individuals with autism spectrum disorder: A meta-analysis. *Research in Autism Spectrum Disorders, 83*, 101759. https://doi.org/10.1016/j.rasd.2021.101759

Thomas Craig, K. J., Khan, R., Hariharaputran, S., Gao, J., & Haber, M. (2025). Real-world evaluation of prevalence, cohort characteristics, and healthcare utilization and expenditures among adults and children with autism spectrum disorder, attention-deficit hyperactivity disorder, or both. *BMC Health Services Research, 25*, 1048. https://doi.org/10.1186/s12913-025-13296-2

Chapter 2

How AuDHD presents in daily life

It's a Tuesday morning and you're standing in the kitchen holding a coffee mug, staring at the bench as though it might contain instructions. Your phone shows eleven unread messages, a calendar reminder for something you've double-booked, and a notification that your grocery delivery has been cancelled because you forgot to update the payment details. Again.

The dishwasher is beeping with the particular insistence of a smoke alarm that has decided everything is an emergency. Your neighbour's dog is barking. The light through the window is doing something aggressive. And your brain, which cannot currently locate your car keys despite the fact that you put them down four minutes ago, is simultaneously replaying a conversation you had with someone called Dave about cricket statistics in 2019 with the fidelity of a court transcript.

This is Tuesday.

Not a crisis. Not a meltdown. Not a bad day. Just the ordinary cognitive weather of an AuDHD brain trying to do the thing that neurotypical people call 'getting ready in the morning,' which they appear to accomplish without the internal experience of running seven applications on hardware designed for three.

If you've picked up this book, chances are you recognised something in that paragraph. The attention that goes everywhere except where you need it. The sensory environment that won't stay in the background where it belongs. The memory system that operates with the filing logic of a library organised by someone who was interrupted every thirty seconds and eventually gave up and sorted everything by colour. Chapter 1 argued that AuDHD is a distinct neurological profile, not two conditions bolted together. This chapter is about what that profile actually does when you set it loose in a kitchen on a Tuesday morning and ask it to find its keys.

THE WALKING CONTRADICTION

The charity Autistica, in their overview of the autism-ADHD intersection, landed on a phrase that most AuDHD adults recognise with the jolt of being unexpectedly understood: 'Being AuDHD sometimes feels like I'm a walking contradiction.' It's a description that has spread through the community precisely because it names an experience the clinical literature has been circling without landing on.

The contradiction goes like this. You crave routine, and you crave novelty. You need structure to function, and the structure bores you to tears within a week.

You build systems with the meticulous precision of someone who genuinely enjoys colour-coded spreadsheets, and then you abandon those systems the moment your ADHD brain notices that maintaining the system has itself become a task requiring executive function you no longer have available because you used it all building the system.

You want deep, predictable relationships and you are impulsive in social situations. You are exhausted by change and under-stimulated by sameness. You are, from the outside, maddeningly inconsistent.

From the inside, though, the contradiction has its own coherence. And understanding that coherence is the key to understanding why AuDHD daily life looks the way it does.

In *Harder than it should be*, I used a computational metaphor for this experience that people kept telling me was the most useful thing in the book, which either means it was genuinely illuminating or the rest of the book set a very low bar.

The metaphor was this: living with AuDHD is like running translation software every waking moment. Your brain receives input from the world in one format and must translate it, in real time, into the format the world expects as output. The translation covers social cues, sensory information, executive demands, emotional regulation, and the performance of normality, all simultaneously, all without visible lag, all while the system that's doing the translating is also managing its own internal contradictions between the need for order and the craving for stimulation.

Neurotypical people don't run translation software. They receive input and respond. The conversion is native. For AuDHD brains, every interaction involves an additional computational step that consumes energy, attention, and cognitive resources that are then unavailable for the actual task. The contradiction that others see from the outside, the inconsistency, the mystifying gap between capability and performance, is what the translation looks like when the system is running low on processing power.

Which is most of the time. Because the software never shuts down.

EXECUTIVE FUNCTION, OR THE CONDUCTOR WHO KEEPS LEAVING THE BUILDING

Executive function is the set of cognitive processes that let you plan, prioritise, organise, initiate, and switch between tasks. It is, in effect, the conductor of the orchestra: the thing that coordinates all the other things into something resembling a coherent performance.

In AuDHD, the conductor has a complicated relationship with the job. Some days, when the music is interesting, the conductor is not merely present but extraordinary, holding complex arrangements together with a focus and intensity that neurotypical conductors can't match. Other days, the conductor wanders off to investigate something more interesting in another building and leaves the brass section and the violins to negotiate their own tempo, with predictably chaotic results.

This is not the same as ADHD executive function difficulty, and the distinction matters. Pure ADHD executive function tends to be unreliable across contexts: everything is harder to initiate, sustain, and organise. Pure autistic executive function tends to be rigid rather than unreliable: initiating and maintaining tasks works well within established routines but breaks down when flexibility is required.

AuDHD executive function is both unreliable and rigid, which sounds like it should be impossible but is in fact simply exhausting. You can't start the task, and once you've started it you can't stop, and switching to a different task feels like being asked to change the engine on a moving car.

I can write for twelve hours. I do this regularly. The capacity for sustained, deep engagement with complex material is one of the genuine gifts of this neurology, and I will fight anyone who tries to pathologise it.

But if you interrupt me at hour six to ask what I'd like for dinner, the cognitive cost of context-switching, of pulling my attention out of the deep channel it's carved for itself and redirecting it toward a question about rice versus noodles, is so disproportionate to the simplicity of the question that I will either not hear you, answer a question you didn't ask, or experience a flash of irritation so intense it startles both of us.

Hương has learned to text me the dinner plan rather than asking. The text sits until the natural break arrives. This accommodation costs nothing, solves everything, and took us approximately eight months of confused arguments to discover.

The grocery shop is where AuDHD executive function goes to die.

What appears to be a simple errand requires the simultaneous deployment of working memory (what do we need), sensory management (fluorescent lights, the particular hell of commercial refrigerator hum, other humans moving unpredictably through narrow spaces), decision-making (seventeen brands of fish sauce, each nearly identical, and the autistic brain wants to compare them all while the ADHD brain wants to grab one and leave immediately), social navigation (queue etiquette, small talk with the cashier, the ambient expectation that you should appear relaxed while performing a task that requires more cognitive resources than most people's entire workday), and time management (you budgeted thirty minutes; your autistic need for completion is arguing with your ADHD need to escape).

I regularly arrive home with three jars of something I already had and none of the thing I went out to buy. This is not absent-mindedness. This is a processing system overwhelmed by the computational demands of an activity that neurotypical brains file under 'easy.'

SENSORY PROCESSING, OR LIVING IN A WORLD WITH THE VOLUME STUCK ON ELEVEN

The sensory experience of AuDHD is paradoxical in a way that makes perfect sense once you understand the profile, and no sense at all if you're trying to understand it through either condition's lens alone. You seek sensation and you avoid sensation. Not alternately. Simultaneously.

Autistic sensory processing tends toward sensitivity: the world is too loud, too bright, too textured, too much. ADHD sensory processing tends toward seeking: the world is not stimulating enough, and the brain craves input the way a cold engine craves fuel. AuDHD sensory processing does both, which means you are a person who craves the deep pressure of a weighted blanket while being driven to genuine distress by the tag in your shirt.

You find the rhythmic sound of rain profoundly calming and the arrhythmic tapping of a pen at the next table intolerable. You seek out the overwhelming visual richness of a Vietnamese market because your ADHD brain lights up with stimulation, and then you spend the next three hours recovering in a dark room because your autistic sensory system has been overloaded by the experience your ADHD brain demanded.

This is the sensory paradox, and it is one of the most misunderstood aspects of AuDHD daily life. Clinicians who understand either autism or ADHD but not the interaction will look at the sensation-seeking and conclude you can't be autistic (because autistic people avoid sensation), or look at the sensory overwhelm and conclude you can't have ADHD (because ADHD people seek sensation). The paradox is the profile.

If your sensory experience makes you feel like a contradiction, you're probably not contradictory. You're probably AuDHD.

The temporal dimension adds complexity. Sensory tolerance is not fixed. It fluctuates with fatigue, stress, emotional state, time of day, allostatic load, and the accumulated sensory debt from earlier in the day. I can walk through a noisy café at 10am and find it pleasantly stimulating. By 3pm, after a day of writing and video calls and the ambient processing demands of existing in a body that never stops translating, the same café at the same volume is intolerable. The café hasn't changed. My processing capacity has. Understanding your own sensory weather, the way your tolerance shifts across the day, is one of the most practically useful things you can learn about your AuDHD brain.

SOCIAL COMMUNICATION, OR THE PERFORMANCE NOBODY ASKED FOR

AuDHD social communication is its own particular theatre. The autistic architecture struggles with the unwritten rules, the implicit expectations, the baffling amount of information that neurotypical people transmit through tone, facial expression, and the precise angle at which they hold their coffee cup during a meeting.

The ADHD architecture adds impulsivity to this already challenging situation, which means you might understand the social rule perfectly well in theory and violate it in practice because the thought arrived and your mouth opened before the social monitoring system had time to review the draft.

The result is a person who prepares for social interactions with the thoroughness of a general planning a military campaign and then ad-libs half the conversation because the ADHD brain found the prepared script boring. You rehearse what you're going to say in the car. You arrive. You say something entirely different. You spend the drive home reviewing the performance with the critical eye of a theatre reviewer who has never given a positive notice.

This is masking, and it is one of the most energy-intensive activities an AuDHD person performs. The word 'masking' makes it sound passive, like putting on a costume. It isn't. Masking is an active, real-time, cognitively demanding performance that requires simultaneously monitoring your own behaviour, reading the room, adjusting your output to match expected norms, suppressing autistic responses that might be visible, channelling ADHD impulses into socially acceptable forms, and maintaining the appearance of ease while doing all of this.

It is the translation software running at full capacity on a task that has no completion point, because social interaction doesn't have a finish line. It just eventually stops, and then you go home and don't speak for three hours because your language processing system has filed for bankruptcy.

The cost of this performance is real and measurable, even if the standard metrics don't measure it. In Chapter 3, we'll look at the research on allostatic load and what chronic masking does to the body over years and decades. For now, it's enough to note that the social 'inconsistency' that others observe in AuDHD people, the person who is charming at a dinner party and non-verbal the following morning, is not inconsistency. It is the difference between a system running at capacity and a system that has run out.

THE EMOTIONAL LANDSCAPE

AuDHD emotions are intense, fast, confusing, and frequently misinterpreted by everyone involved, including the person having them.

Autistic emotional processing tends to be deep but slow. The feeling arrives, sits in the body, and may take hours or days to become legible. You know something is happening emotionally but you can't name it yet. ADHD emotional processing is fast and intense. The feeling arrives, fills the room, and may be gone by the time you've worked out what it was. AuDHD combines both patterns, which means you experience emotions with ADHD intensity and autistic processing lag, producing a lived experience in which you are flooded by a feeling you can't identify, can't regulate, can't articulate, and may not fully understand until much later when you're doing something else entirely and the interpretation arrives like a letter that was posted three days ago.

Rejection sensitivity deserves its own mention because it is one of the most common and least understood features of the AuDHD emotional landscape. The term 'rejection sensitive dysphoria' (RSD) describes the intense, often overwhelming emotional response to perceived rejection or criticism.

Perceived is the operative word. The rejection does not need to be real. It needs to be processed as real by a nervous system that is simultaneously hyper-alert to social threat (the autistic monitoring system) and emotionally hair-trigger (the ADHD intensity). A colleague's ambiguous email. A friend's delayed response to a message. A partner's facial expression during a conversation.

Any of these can trigger an emotional cascade that feels catastrophic and is, to the person experiencing it, genuinely painful, not metaphorically painful. The pain is as real as a burn. It's just not visible, which means it is routinely dismissed by people who can't see it and misdiagnosed by clinicians who interpret it as anxiety, borderline personality disorder, or melodrama.

I've learned to say to Hương, 'I'm having a feeling I can't identify yet.' This sounds absurd in most therapeutic models, where emotional literacy is treated as a basic competency. But it is accurate. The feeling is real. The identification is pending.

The lag between experience and understanding is a feature of the system, not a failure of emotional intelligence. AuDHD people often have extraordinary emotional intelligence about other people's feelings while remaining genuinely confused by their own, which is exactly what you'd expect from a system that runs translation software for external input but has no native format for internal data.

WHAT THIS COSTS, BEFORE YOU NOTICE IT COSTING ANYTHING

Here's the thing about everything I've described in this chapter. All of it is invisible. All of it is happening behind a performance of normality that most AuDHD adults have spent their entire lives perfecting. The executive function negotiation, the sensory management, the social translation, the emotional processing, all of it runs in the background while the person appears to be simply 'getting on with things.'

The energy cost of this invisible labour is enormous. By mid-afternoon on a typical day, I have processed more sensory information, performed more social translations, made more executive function negotiations, and managed more emotional weather than most neurotypical people process in a week. This is not an exaggeration.

It is what the computational metaphor predicts and what the lived experience confirms: the translation software runs continuously, it consumes significant resources, and the body keeps a tab.

The tab comes due. It always comes due. Sometimes it comes due as a shutdown: the system goes quiet, language becomes effortful, and you retreat to a dark room and don't want to be spoken to.

Sometimes it comes due as a meltdown: the system overwhelms, the emotional regulation you've been maintaining all day collapses, and you cry or rage or both in a way that is entirely disproportionate to whatever triggered it, because the trigger isn't the cause. The trigger is the last grain of sand on a pile that's been accumulating since you opened your eyes that morning and the dishwasher started beeping.

And sometimes the tab comes due slowly, over years and decades, as the chronic invisible labour of performing neurotypicality accumulates in the body as allostatic load: the physiological cost of sustained stress that standard blood tests don't capture and standard clinical models don't account for. That slow accumulation, and what the research is beginning to reveal about its consequences, is the subject of Chapter 3.

It is the chapter that scares me. I think it might need to.

REFERENCES

Autistica. (2025). ADHD and autism. *Autistica.* https://www.autistica.org.uk/what-is-autism/adhd-and-autism

Hopkins, L. (2026). *Harder than it should be: Why everything is more exhausting than it used to be and what your brain needs you to know about it.* degrees138.

Raymaker, D. M., Teo, A. R., Steckler, N. A., Lentz, B., Scharer, M., Delos Santos, A., Kapp, S. K., Hunter, M., Joyce, A., & Nicolaidis, C. (2020). "Having all of your internal resources exhausted beyond measure and being left with no clean-up crew": Defining autistic burnout. *Autism in Adulthood, 2*(2), 132–143. https://doi.org/10.1089/aut.2019.0079

Rong, Y., Yang, C.-J., Jin, Y., & Wang, Y. (2021). Prevalence of attention-deficit/hyperactivity disorder in individuals with autism spectrum disorder: A meta-analysis. *Research in Autism Spectrum Disorders, 83*, 101759. https://doi.org/10.1016/j.rasd.2021.101759

Thomas Craig, K. J., Khan, R., Hariharaputran, S., Gao, J., & Haber, M. (2025). Real-world evaluation of prevalence, cohort characteristics, and healthcare utilization and expenditures among adults and children with autism spectrum disorder, attention-deficit hyperactivity disorder, or both. *BMC Health Services Research, 25*, 1048. https://doi.org/10.1186/s12913-025-13296-2

Chapter 3

The invisible toll: AuDHD, allostatic load, and what it costs the body

On Monday 9 February 2026, I played tennis, ate dinner at an Italian restaurant in Đà Lạt, and wrote a gushing Google review of the meal.

I remember none of it. Not the tennis, not the food, not the review. I have photographic evidence of the dinner and a five-star review under my name that reads like someone having a lovely evening. From the outside, I *was* having a lovely evening. From the inside—as I later reconstructed from the wreckage—nobody was home.

Two days later, the headache that had been building for ten months became a permanent resident. My blood pressure spiked to 170 over 89. I presented to the emergency department of my local hospital, where the doctor glanced at my AI-translated Vietnamese-language medical summary, laughed, and walked away. I went home with a 9-out-of-10 headache, no pain medication, and the dawning recognition that whatever was happening in my body had exceeded the capacity of the local medical system to detect, let alone treat.

My quarterly blood panels, for the record, were normal. They'd been normal for months. They would continue to be normal through weeks of escalating symptoms that included chronic fatigue so severe that one hour of activity required several hours of recovery, widespread body pain with myofascial trigger points that made my massage therapist's eyes widen, brain fog, balance difficulties, and the persistent, immovable headache that no analgesic could touch and no scan could explain.

I documented the collapse and its aftermath in *The body remembers the fire*, and I'll draw on that account here. But the story I want to tell in this chapter is not the personal one. It's the story of what was happening underneath the symptoms—the physiological process the blood tests weren't designed to capture, the research that explains why, and the implications that kept me awake at 2am once I started assembling the picture.

The picture is this: sixty-six years of undiagnosed AuDHD had produced a cumulative physiological burden that the research literature calls allostatic load. My body had been paying a biological surcharge for decades of masking, sensory overload, executive function taxation, chronic social stress, and the particular metabolic expense of performing neurotypicality without a diagnosis, without support, and without anyone—including me—understanding what the performance was costing. The symptoms that baffled my local hospital were not separate problems. They were the body's invoice, delivered all at once, for a debt that had been accumulating since childhood.

What you ignore does not disappear. It relocates.

THE ALLOSTATIC LOAD EVIDENCE

Allostatic load is the cumulative physiological cost of chronic stress. The concept was developed by Bruce McEwen and Eliot Stellar in 1993, and it describes something deceptively simple: when the body's stress response systems are activated repeatedly without adequate recovery, the machinery of stress itself begins to cause damage. The hormones meant to protect you in emergencies—cortisol, adrenaline, the full fight-or-flight cascade—become toxic when they run continuously. The system designed to save your life in a crisis slowly degrades the body it's trying to protect.

In 2023, a team at Columbia University led by Martin Picard published findings that gave allostatic load a cellular price tag. Bobba-Alves and colleagues found that chronic glucocorticoid exposure—the cellular equivalent of sustained cortisol stress—increased cellular energy expenditure by approximately 60% and accelerated biological aging as measured by DNA methylation clocks and telomere shortening (Bobba-Alves et al., 2023). Sixty percent. That's the metabolic surcharge of a body running on chronic stress. Nobody gets a bill for it. The body pays anyway.

A 2026 study confirmed that financial strain and everyday discrimination—two experiences that are statistically overrepresented in neurodivergent populations—are associated with accelerated epigenetic aging across the lifespan (Ciciurkaite et al., 2026). A 2025 neuroimaging study found that allostatic load scores were linked to structural brain changes in regions sensitive to aging, including the hippocampus and prefrontal cortex (Palix et al., 2025). These are the structures central to memory, emotional regulation, and executive function—the very capacities that AuDHD people are already working harder to maintain.

Now map those findings onto a life spent navigating neurotypical systems with an AuDHD brain. The masking. The sensory management. The executive function taxation. The social translation running continuously in the background. The financial instability that follows executive function differences through every career decision. Every one of those experiences generates exactly the kind of chronic, unrelieved stress that the allostatic load research identifies as biologically damaging. And unlike a single traumatic event, which produces a spike of stress that the body can process and recover from, the stress of undiagnosed AuDHD is ambient. It doesn't have peaks and troughs. It has a floor, and the floor is higher than most bodies are designed to sustain indefinitely.

Raymaker and colleagues defined this in 2020 as autistic burnout: a distinct syndrome resulting from chronic mismatch between expectations and capacity, characterised by pervasive exhaustion, loss of previously reliable skills, and reduced sensory tolerance (Raymaker et al., 2020). What Raymaker's work captures from the lived-experience side, the allostatic load research captures from the cellular side. They're describing the same phenomenon from different altitudes. The person feels the exhaustion, the skill loss, the narrowing of what's tolerable. The cells are running 60% above normal energy expenditure, shortening their telomeres, and aging faster than the calendar says they should.

A real-world study of 2.3 million insurance members found that the health profile of people with both autism and ADHD was synergistically different from either condition alone—not additive, synergistic (Thomas Craig et al., 2025). The combination produces worse health outcomes than the sum of its parts would predict. I wonder whether that synergistic burden is what allostatic load looks like from the perspective of an insurance database: the statistical shadow of millions of bodies paying a surcharge nobody measured.

THE LIFE EXPECTANCY GAP NOBODY HAS STUDIED

In January 2025, O'Nions and colleagues published the first UK study to use the life-table method to estimate life expectancy for adults with diagnosed ADHD (O'Nions et al., 2025). Using data from 30,000 adults across 792 general practices, they found life expectancy reductions of 4.5 to 9 years for men and 6.5 to 11 years for women. The authors noted, with appropriate caution, that diagnosed adults may overrepresent those with additional health conditions, potentially inflating the estimates. Even at the conservative end, the gap is substantial.

The autism mortality research shows larger reductions. Hirvikoski and colleagues, in their landmark 2016 Swedish study of 27,000 autistic individuals, found premature mortality was markedly increased across a multitude of medical conditions, with the strongest effects among women and those with intellectual disabilities (Hirvikoski et al., 2016).

The AuDHD-specific life expectancy gap—the one that would tell me what having both conditions together actually costs—has never been studied. Given the Thomas Craig finding that the combination is synergistically rather than additively harmful, I wonder what that number looks like. I wonder whether anyone is designing the study. I wonder why they aren't.

I wrote about this gap in *Misdiagnosed*, in a chapter I called 'The life expectancy question.' What strikes me now, rereading it, is how much of my anger at the time was directed at the absence of the research rather than at any particular finding. The data doesn't exist because nobody has prioritised collecting it. The absence is not an accident. It is a statement about whose health outcomes the research establishment considers worth measuring.

THE DEMENTIA EVIDENCE

The allostatic load research was sobering. What follows is worse.

A 2023 Israeli cohort study followed 109,218 people over a mean of 17.2 years. Dementia occurred in 13.2% of those with adult ADHD, compared to 7.0% without. After adjusting for 18 potential confounders, the hazard ratio was 2.77—nearly three times the risk. Notably, psychostimulant medication appeared to reduce the association, raising the possibility that treatment may be protective (Levine et al., 2023).

A Swedish registry study of 3.59 million individuals found an ADHD hazard ratio for dementia of 2.92 and for mild cognitive impairment of 6.21. Adjustment for psychiatric comorbidities attenuated the dementia figure to 1.62, but it remained significant (Dobrosavljevic et al., 2022). A 2024 Argentine study—small but mechanistically striking—found a hazard ratio of 54.54 for Lewy body dementia specifically in the ADHD cohort (Golimstok et al.,

2024). That confidence interval is wide enough to drive a truck through, but the dopaminergic pathway makes biological sense: both ADHD and Lewy body dementia involve disruption to the same neurotransmitter systems.

The autism evidence is equally sobering. A 2021 Medicaid study found autistic adults approximately 2.6 times more likely to be diagnosed with early-onset dementia than the general population (Vivanti et al., 2021). A 2025 follow-up using linked Medicare and Medicaid data from over 114,000 autistic adults found that among those over 64, 35.1% carried a dementia diagnosis, versus approximately 10 to 11% in the general population (Vivanti et al., 2025). I need you to sit with that number. More than a third. Among autistic adults over 64 in this dataset, more than one in three had been diagnosed with dementia.

A Swedish family study found elevated dementia risk not only in autistic people but in their biological relatives, suggesting shared genetic and developmental pathways rather than purely environmental causation (Zhang et al., 2025). And a 2025 Geneva University study identified the first plausible neurobiological mechanism: altered iron distribution in the brains of adults with ADHD, correlated with elevated neurofilament light chain protein—a marker of neuronal damage seen in early-stage dementias (Berberat et al., 2025).

The 2023 International Summit on Intellectual Disability and Dementia produced a consensus document identifying a problem that connects directly to the diagnostic challenges described in Chapter 1: overlapping symptoms of autism and dementia create a critical barrier to accurate diagnosis (Janicki et al., 2025). Executive function decline, increased rigidity, memory difficulties, heightened anxiety—these are features of both conditions.

Clinicians may interpret early dementia symptoms in an autistic person as 'just their autism.' The diagnostic overshadowing that delayed my own AuDHD recognition for forty years may be operating again, this time hiding cognitive decline behind a neurodevelopmental label.

I wonder how many people that's already happened to.

THE STRUCTURAL HARM ARGUMENT

Here is where I need to be careful, and here is where I need to be honest, and the two requirements are pulling in different directions.

I am not arguing that AuDHD causes dementia. The research does not support that claim and neither do I. What I am arguing—and what Bridgette Hamstead articulated in her March 2026 synthesis with more clarity than any peer-reviewed journal has attempted—is that elevated dementia risk in neurodivergent populations may be, in significant part, the biological record of what a lifetime of structural exclusion does to a brain over time.

The mechanism is allostatic load. Chronic HPA axis activation and the associated immune-inflammatory response damage the hippocampus, the amygdala, and the prefrontal cortex—the structures most vulnerable to Alzheimer's pathology. Chronic stress doesn't just feel bad. It erodes the hardware. And the stress of undiagnosed, unsupported AuDHD is not acute stress that arrives and passes. It is the ambient, unrelieved, structurally produced stress of navigating every waking hour in environments designed for a different neurology, without accommodation, without recognition, and frequently without the language to explain to yourself why everything is so much harder than it appears to be for everyone else.

Sleep disruption is prevalent in both autistic people and people with ADHD, and sleep quality is one of the most robustly established modifiable risk factors for Alzheimer's disease. The glymphatic system—the brain's waste-clearing mechanism—operates primarily during deep sleep, clearing the beta-amyloid and tau protein accumulations associated with neurodegeneration. If your sleep architecture is disrupted by sensory sensitivity, by the hypervigilance that comes with chronic masking, by the circadian rhythm differences common in ADHD, or by the simple fact that your nervous system doesn't stand down when the lights go off, then the waste-clearing process is compromised. Night after night. Year after year. Decade after decade.

Hamstead's framing is important: the research should be read not as evidence of inherent neurological fragility, but as evidence of structural harm made visible at the cellular level. Parts of the neurodiversity movement, in an understandable rush to destigmatise, have sometimes minimised the medical realities of neurodivergent life. And the medical establishment, in its habitual focus on individual pathology, has sometimes failed to see the structural forces producing the pathology. Both positions are incomplete. Destigmatising neurodivergence and taking its physical health consequences seriously are not contradictory. They are both acts of care.

MY OWN BODY AS EVIDENCE

When I presented to FV Hospital in Ho Chi Minh City in early March 2026, I framed the clinical reasoning around allostatic load. I cited van der Kolk, McEwen, and Raymaker in my referral letter. I explained that sixty-six years of undiagnosed neurodivergence had required chronic masking and autonomic hypervigilance, resulting in sustained HPA axis activation and cumulative physiological damage. I requested cortisol rhythm testing, extended thyroid panels, inflammatory markers, iron studies, coagulation profiles, and autonomic assessment.

I also flagged a drug interaction between my clopidogrel and escitalopram that increases bleeding risk—a combination I'd been on for months that nobody had connected to the unexplained bruising. This is what healthcare looks like for an AuDHD person who happens to have clinical training: you do the clinician's differential diagnosis yourself, because the system wasn't designed to do it for you.

The comprehensive results confirmed no acute pathology. A medication review resolved the ten-month headache. I feel healthier now than I have in decades. But here's the thing that stays with me: the headache wasn't structural. The pain wasn't orthopaedic. The fatigue wasn't laziness. They were the body's response to cumulative, unrelieved allostatic strain—exactly what the Bobba-Alves research would predict in a system running 60% above normal energy expenditure without anyone accounting for the metabolic cost. My quarterly blood panels were normal because quarterly blood panels don't ask the right questions about a neurodivergent body.

I am, in this respect, my own Chapter 3.

WHAT TO DO WITH FRIGHTENING INFORMATION

I have a responsibility, having laid out this evidence, to do something other than leave you frightened. So here's what I think matters practically.

Allostatic load is modifiable. That is the most important sentence in this chapter. Environmental change reduces allostatic load. I moved to Vietnam and my depression vanished within months. Same brain. Different environment. Same pension. Different cost of living. The body responded to the change in circumstances, not to a change in medication. Accurate diagnosis reduces allostatic load. Understanding at sixty-six that I was neurodivergent, not broken, reframed decades of suffering from personal failure to systemic mismatch. Stopping the performance of neurotypicality reduces allostatic load. Unmasking, imperfectly and gradually, is the single most important thing I've done for my body since arriving in this country.

The finding that stimulant medication may be protective against dementia needs honest discussion. It appeared in the Levine et al. Israeli cohort and is mechanistically plausible: if the ADHD-dementia link involves dopaminergic dysregulation, medication that normalises dopaminergic function may reduce the downstream risk. This does not mean everyone with ADHD should immediately seek stimulant medication. It means the conversation about medication needs to include long-term neuroprotective considerations that most prescribers aren't currently discussing.

Sleep quality deserves more clinical attention than it receives. If the glymphatic waste-clearing system operates primarily during deep sleep, and if AuDHD sleep is structurally disrupted by sensory sensitivity, circadian differences, and autonomic hypervigilance, then sleep intervention is not a lifestyle recommendation. It is a neurological priority. Ask your GP about sleep architecture. If they look blank, that tells you something about the state of the field.

And ask for the blood work that matters. Cardiovascular markers. Inflammatory markers. Iron studies. Cortisol rhythm testing if available. The standard quarterly panel was not designed for a body running chronic allostatic overload, and normal results from a test that doesn't measure the right things should not be confused with evidence that you're fine.

I wonder what it costs a body to spend fifty years pretending to be someone else.

I wonder whether the medical establishment will take this seriously before the generation of late-diagnosed AuDHD adults—the ones who spent their entire working lives undiagnosed and unsupported—reaches the age where the consequences become undeniable.

I wonder whether destigmatising neurodivergence and taking its physical health consequences seriously might turn out to be the same project, not competing ones.

The next chapter is about executive function tools and strategies, which sounds like a gear change after this one. It isn't. Every strategy that reduces cognitive load, every accommodation that makes daily life less metabolically expensive, every tool that lets an AuDHD brain work with its architecture rather than against it, is also an intervention against allostatic load. The practical chapters that follow are not separate from the argument this chapter has made. They are the response to it.

REFERENCES

Berberat, J., Kagerer, S. M., Späni, C., Hua, J., Bavato, F., Gruber, P., van Zijl, P. C., Perroud, N., Li, X., Stämpfli, P., Seifritz, E., Lövblad, K.-O., Quednow, B. B., & Unschuld, P. G. (2025). Brain iron load and neuroaxonal vulnerability in adult attention-deficit hyperactivity disorder. *Psychiatry and Clinical Neurosciences, 79*(5), 282–289. https://doi.org/10.1111/pcn.13806

Bobba-Alves, N., Sturm, G., Lin, J., Ware, S. A., Karan, K. R., Monzel, A. S., Bris, C., Procaccio, V., Lenaers, G., Higgins-Chen, A., Levine, M., Horvath, S., Santhanam, B. S., Kaufman, B. A., Hirano, M., Epel, E., & Picard, M. (2023). Cellular allostatic load is linked to increased energy expenditure and accelerated biological aging. *Psychoneuroendocrinology, 155*, 106322. https://doi.org/10.1016/j.psyneuen.2023.106322

Ciciurkaite, G., Peng, S., Mitchell, C., Perry, B. L., & Lee, B. (2026). Psychosocial stressors, accelerated biological aging, and multiple morbidities: Evidence from an age-diverse sample. *PLOS ONE*. https://doi.org/10.1371/journal.pone.0343987

Dobrosavljevic, M., Solares, C., Cortese, S., Andershed, H., & Larsson, H. (2022). Attention-deficit/hyperactivity disorder as a risk factor for dementia and mild cognitive impairment: A population-based register study. *European Psychiatry, 65*(1), e2. https://doi.org/10.1192/j.eurpsy.2021.2261

Golimstok, Á., García Basalo, M. J., Majul, M., Buonanotte, W., Rojas, M., Campos Fein, M., & Eichel, R. (2024). Adult attention deficit-hyperactivity disorder is associated with Lewy body disease and cognitive impairment: A prospective cohort study with 15-year follow-up. *The American Journal of Geriatric Psychiatry, 32*(10), 1220–1230. https://doi.org/10.1016/j.jagp.2024.04.016

Hirvikoski, T., Mittendorfer-Rutz, E., Boman, M., Larsson, H., Lichtenstein, P., & Bölte, S. (2016). Premature mortality in autism spectrum disorder. *The British Journal of Psychiatry, 208*(3), 232–238. https://doi.org/10.1192/bjp.bp.114.160192

Hopkins, L. (2026). *The body remembers the fire*. degrees138.

Hopkins, L. (2026). *Misdiagnosed: When psychiatry mistakes neurodivergence for mental illness*. degrees138.

Janicki, M. P., McCallion, P., Jokinen, N., Service, K. P., Mughal, D. T., Watchman, K., Gomiero, T., Larsen, F. K., & Keller, S. M. (2025). Autism, diagnostics, and dementia: A consensus report from the 2nd International Summit on Intellectual Disabilities and Dementia. *International Journal of Geriatric Psychiatry, 40*(6), e70110. https://doi.org/10.1002/gps.70110

Levine, S. Z., Rotstein, A., Kodesh, A., Sandin, S., Lee, B. K., Weinstein, G., Schnaider Beeri, M., & Reichenberg, A. (2023). Adult attention-deficit/hyperactivity disorder and the risk of dementia. *JAMA Network Open, 6*(10), e2338088. https://doi.org/10.1001/jamanetworkopen.2023.38088

McEwen, B. S., & Stellar, E. (1993). Stress and the individual: Mechanisms leading to disease. *Archives of Internal Medicine, 153*(18), 2093–2101. https://doi.org/10.1001/archinte.1993.00410180039004

O'Nions, E., El Baou, C., John, A., Lewer, D., Mandy, W., McKechnie, D. G. J., Petersen, I., & Stott, J. (2025). Life expectancy and years of life lost for adults with diagnosed ADHD in the UK: Matched cohort study. *The British Journal of Psychiatry, 226*(5), 261–268. https://doi.org/10.1192/bjp.2024.199

Palix, C., Chauveau, L., Felisatti, F., Chocat, A., Coulbault, L., Hébert, O., Mézenge, F., Landeau, B., Haudry, S., Fauvel, S., Collette, F., Klimecki, O., Marchant, N. L., De La Sayette, V., Vivien, D., Chételat, G., Poisnel, G., & the Medit-Ageing Research Group. (2025). Allostatic load, a measure of cumulative physiological stress, impairs brain structure but not β-accumulation in older adults: An exploratory study. *Frontiers in Aging Neuroscience, 17*, 1508677. https://doi.org/10.3389/fnagi.2025.1508677

Raymaker, D. M., Teo, A. R., Steckler, N. A., Lentz, B., Scharer, M., Delos Santos, A., Kapp, S. K., Hunter, M., Joyce, A., & Nicolaidis, C. (2020). "Having all of your internal resources exhausted beyond measure and being left with no clean-up crew": Defining autistic burnout. *Autism in Adulthood, 2*(2), 132–143. https://doi.org/10.1089/aut.2019.0079

Thomas Craig, K. J., Khan, R., Hariharaputran, S., Gao, J., & Haber, M. (2025). Real-world evaluation of prevalence, cohort characteristics, and healthcare utilization and expenditures among adults and children with autism spectrum disorder, attention-deficit hyperactivity disorder, or both. *BMC Health Services Research, 25*, 1048. https://doi.org/10.1186/s12913-025-13296-2

Vivanti, G., Tao, S., Lyall, K., Robins, D. L., & Shea, L. L. (2021). The prevalence and incidence of early-onset dementia among adults with autism spectrum disorder. *Autism Research, 14*(10), 2189–2199. https://doi.org/10.1002/aur.2590

Vivanti, G., Lee, W. L., Ventimiglia, J., Tao, S., Lyall, K., & Shea, L. L. (2025). Prevalence of dementia among US adults with autism spectrum disorder. *JAMA Network Open, 8*(1), e2453691. https://doi.org/10.1001/jamanetworkopen.2024.53691

Zhang, L., et al. (2025). Association between autism and dementia across generations: Evidence from a family study of the Swedish population. *Molecular Psychiatry*. https://doi.org/10.1038/s41380-025-03045-6

Chapter 4

Executive function tools and strategies

I lost my reading glasses three times while writing this chapter. The third time, they were on my head. I mention this not as a charming anecdote about absent-mindedness but as field notes from the condition the chapter is about.

Executive function difficulty in AuDHD is not an occasional inconvenience. It is the weather. You don't get days off from it. You get days where the weather is slightly less catastrophic and you mistake them for competence.

In *It's the circumstances*, I argued that individual coping strategies are a poor substitute for environmental change. I stand by that. The most effective executive function intervention I've ever experienced was moving to a country where the cost of living meant I could stop worrying about money, which freed up approximately 40% of the cognitive bandwidth I'd been spending on financial survival. No app does that. No planner does that. No amount of colour-coded task management replaces the executive function that poverty steals.

But. We live in the world we live in, not the one we'd design if anyone asked. And within that world, there are strategies that genuinely reduce the daily executive function tax on an AuDHD brain. This chapter is about those strategies. None of them will fix the underlying neurology, because the neurology doesn't need fixing —it needs accommodating. What follows is a set of accommodations that have survived contact with my own brain and the brains of my clients, which is a higher bar than most executive function advice clears.

THE PROBLEM NOBODY NAMES CORRECTLY

Most executive function advice is written for ADHD brains or autistic brains, not AuDHD brains. The distinction matters enormously.

ADHD executive function advice focuses on initiation and sustained attention: how to start tasks, how to stay on them, how to resist distraction. It assumes the problem is getting the engine running and keeping it running.

Autistic executive function advice focuses on flexibility and transitions: how to shift between tasks, how to handle unexpected changes, how to tolerate the discomfort of broken routines. It assumes the problem is steering.

AuDHD executive function involves both problems simultaneously, which means the ADHD advice to 'just start anywhere' collides with the autistic need to start in the right place, and the autistic advice to 'create a routine' collides with the ADHD tendency to abandon any routine the moment it becomes boring—which in my experience takes approximately four to seven days. The standard advice for either condition, applied to AuDHD, has the success rate of a dating profile that describes two entirely different people and hopes someone will find both of them attractive.

The computational metaphor from *Harder than it should be* is useful here. AuDHD executive function is like building the scaffolding and climbing it at the same time. You need the structure (autistic requirement) but you have to construct it on the fly (ADHD reality) because the pre-built structures don't fit your architecture. Every AuDHD person I've worked with has, consciously or not, developed their own scaffolding system. The question is whether that system was designed intentionally or cobbled together from whatever was lying around during a crisis. Most of us are living in the cobbled version.

EXTERNALISE EVERYTHING YOUR BRAIN WON'T HOLD

Russell Barkley, one of the most influential ADHD researchers alive, has spent decades arguing that the core clinical intervention for ADHD is externalisation: moving executive functions out of the mind and into the environment (Barkley, 2012). Make the invisible visible. Put the information where your eyes will land on it rather than where your memory is supposed to retrieve it. Trust the environment more than you trust your recall.

For AuDHD, this principle needs a modification. Externalise, yes, but externalise into systems that are stable enough to satisfy the autistic need for predictability and flexible enough to survive the ADHD need for novelty. This is the razor's edge that every AuDHD organisation system walks, and it's why most off-the-shelf productivity systems fail within a fortnight. They're either too rigid (the ADHD brain rebels) or too flexible (the autistic brain panics).

What works, in my clinical experience and my personal disaster-management programme, is a two-layer system. The first layer is fixed and non-negotiable: the things that must happen regardless of mood, energy, or interest level. For me, this is medication, hydration, and one meal before midday. Three items. Not fifteen. Not a morning routine that reads like a boot camp schedule designed by someone who has never met a nervous system. Three things, externalised onto a whiteboard next to the kettle where my eyes land every morning whether I want them to or not.

The second layer is modular: a rotating set of tools, apps, and approaches that you use until they stop working and then replace without guilt. The AuDHD community calls this 'rotating compensatory strategies,' which is a fancy way of saying: the planner worked for three weeks and now it doesn't, so I'm switching to sticky notes until those stop working too, and this is not failure. This is the system working as designed, for a brain that requires novelty to maintain engagement. The guilt about abandoning systems is more damaging than the abandoned systems themselves. I have a graveyard of productivity apps on my phone. Each one served its purpose. None of them lasted. The graveyard is evidence of adaptation, not incompetence.

BODY DOUBLING AND THE SCIENCE OF NOT BEING ALONE

Body doubling is the practice of doing a task in the presence of another person. The other person doesn't need to help. They don't need to supervise. They just need to be there. For reasons that neuroscience is only beginning to explain, the mere presence of another human body in the room can reduce the executive function barrier to initiating and sustaining tasks that an AuDHD brain finds impossible to start alone.

The evidence base is catching up with what the community has known for years. Eagle and colleagues published a 2024 investigation of body doubling with neurodivergent participants and found it effective for task initiation and completion, with participants describing it as something they had 'naturally found worked and heard about later' (Eagle et al., 2024).

A 2025 VR study by Ara and colleagues found that participants with ADHD completed tasks faster and reported greater sustained attention when working alongside either a human or an AI body double compared to working alone (Ara et al., 2025).

The mechanism likely involves co-regulation—the nervous system borrowing regulatory capacity from another nervous system in proximity, a process Daniel Siegel describes as interpersonal neurobiology (Siegel, 2012).

I draft books, blog posts, articles, YouTube scripts, etc., better in cafés than in my office. This is not about the coffee, though the coffee helps. It's about the ambient human presence: other bodies engaged in their own tasks, providing a low-level regulatory signal that my nervous system uses to stay anchored. I am, without knowing it, body doubling with strangers.

Hương serves the same function at home. When she's in the next room doing her own work, I can sustain focus on administrative tasks that would defeat me entirely if I were alone in the house. She's not helping. She's not even aware she's doing anything. She's being a body in proximity, and my nervous system is using her presence as scaffolding.

For readers without a convenient Hương, virtual body doubling has become widely available through online platforms where neurodivergent people co-work via video call. You turn on your camera, mute your microphone, and work alongside strangers who are doing the same thing. It sounds absurd. It works with a reliability that should embarrass every productivity guru who ever told you the problem was your mindset.

THE INITIATION PROBLEM AND THE DOPAMINE BRIDGE

Task initiation is the AuDHD executive function challenge that causes the most practical damage. You know what needs doing. You may even want to do it. You cannot start. The gap between intention and action is not motivational. It is neurological. The dopaminergic activation required to bridge 'I should do this' and 'I am doing this' is not reliably available on demand in an AuDHD brain.

The most effective initiation strategy I've found is what the community calls a dopamine bridge: never try to move from a high-dopamine activity to a zero-dopamine activity in one step. If you've been writing for two hours and need to do the dishes, the transition from deep engagement to washing-up is a neurological cliff. The dopamine bridge is anything that provides enough stimulation to keep the ADHD brain engaged while the autistic brain handles the sensory and procedural demands of the task. Music works. Podcasts work. Having a conversation on speakerphone works. The key is that the bridge provides novelty and stimulation without requiring executive function, so the available executive function can be directed at the task itself.

I clean the kitchen while listening to neuroscience podcasts. The irony of learning about prefrontal cortex function while scrubbing my coffee pot is not lost on me, but the combination works because the podcast feeds the ADHD need for stimulation while the cleaning satisfies the autistic need for order. Neither activity alone would be sustainable. Together, they negotiate a truce that my executive function system can live with.

DECISION FATIGUE AND THE ART OF DECIDING LESS

Every decision you make in a day costs executive function. Neurotypical brains manage this through automation: they make many small decisions on autopilot, reserving conscious deliberation for the big ones. AuDHD brains automate poorly.

The autistic architecture wants to evaluate every option thoroughly because incomplete evaluation feels unsafe. The ADHD architecture generates more options than any evaluation process can handle because every possibility is interesting for approximately three seconds. The combination means that choosing what to eat for lunch can consume the same executive function resources that a neurotypical person spends on a mid-career job change.

The intervention is radical simplification. Reduce the number of decisions your brain has to make each day by making as many as possible in advance, when you have capacity, rather than in the moment, when you don't. I have hired a cook and eat the same breakfast every day. Not because I lack culinary imagination—although my inability to cook is not a lifestyle choice but is a neurological feature—but because removing that decision at 11am—when my executive function is still warming up and my autistic brain is still adjusting to the fact that the day has had the audacity to begin—saves resources for the decisions that actually matter.

This is not deprivation. This is engineering. Formula 1 teams don't let the driver choose the tyre compound mid-race based on how they're feeling. They decide in advance, based on data, and free the driver to focus on driving. Your daily life can work the same way: pre-decide the things that don't need real-time evaluation, and protect your executive function for the things that do. Meal planning, clothing selection, daily routines, regular purchases—all of these are candidates for pre-decision. The energy you save is not trivial. Over a week, it is the difference between arriving at Friday with something left in the tank and arriving at Friday as a cognitive husk wondering why you can't form sentences. Why do tech bros all wear the same black t-shirt uniform, day in day out? You have your answer.

TIME BLINDNESS AND THE ART OF THE TRANSITION

AuDHD time perception is a distinct cognitive experience that the clinical literature calls time blindness but which might more accurately be called time inconsistency. Time does not flow at a constant rate for an AuDHD brain. It compresses during hyperfocus and expands during boredom. Two hours of writing feels like twenty minutes. Twenty minutes of waiting feels like geological time. The result is chronic lateness, missed deadlines, and the bewildering experience of running out of day before you've run out of tasks, despite having been 'busy' since you opened your eyes.

Timers help more than schedules. A schedule tells you what to do at what time, which requires you to track time accurately—the very skill that's impaired. A timer tells you when time is up, which externalises the tracking to a device that doesn't have dopamine issues. I use timers for everything: writing blocks, phone use, hydration intervals. My phone contains more active timers than some air traffic control systems, and this is not a joke. It is a prosthetic for a cognitive function that my neurology doesn't reliably provide.

Transitions between tasks are where AuDHD executive function most visibly collapses. The autistic brain resists leaving the current activity because the current activity is known. The ADHD brain resists leaving if the current activity is interesting, because switching away from dopamine is neurologically painful in a way that people who haven't experienced it routinely dismiss as laziness. The best transition strategy I've found is the five-minute warning. Tell the AuDHD brain what's coming before it arrives. 'In five minutes, I'm going to stop writing and take Deefer, my yellow Labrador, for a walk.' Say it out loud. Set a timer. When the timer sounds, you have a bridge rather than an ambush.

SMALL MERCIES, LARGE RETURNS

Executive function strategies can sound trivial. Timers. Whiteboards. Podcasts while doing the dishes. Compared to the allostatic load evidence in Chapter 3, these feel like small-bore interventions.

They aren't. Every strategy that reduces cognitive load is also an intervention against allostatic load. Every accommodation that lets an AuDHD brain work with its architecture rather than fighting it reduces the metabolic cost of the day. The Bobba-Alves finding that chronic stress increases cellular energy expenditure by 60% means that anything that reduces the ambient stress of daily functioning is a health intervention, whether it looks like one or not. A whiteboard next to the kettle is not a productivity hack. It is a small act of mercy toward a nervous system that has been compensating at capacity for decades.

The next chapter covers sensory management and environmental design, which is the other half of the same project: arranging the world so that your nervous system can stop working quite so hard to survive it.

REFERENCES

Ara, Z., Rahim, I. B., Zhou, P., Yu, L., Esmaeili, B., Yu, L.-F., & Hong, S. R. (2025). You are not alone: Designing body doubling for ADHD in virtual reality. *Proceedings of the ACM.* https://doi.org/10.48550/arXiv.2509.12153

Barkley, R. A. (2012). *Executive functions: What they are, how they work, and why they evolved.* Guilford Press.

Bobba-Alves, N., Sturm, G., Lin, J., Ware, S. A., Karan, K. R., Monzel, A. S., Bris, C., Procaccio, V., Lenaers, G., Higgins-Chen, A., Levine, M., Horvath, S., Santhanam, B. S., Kaufman, B. A., Hirano, M., Epel, E., & Picard, M. (2023). Cellular allostatic load is linked to increased energy expenditure and accelerated biological aging. *Psychoneuroendocrinology, 155,* 106322. https://doi.org/10.1016/j.psyneuen.2023.106322

Eagle, T., et al. (2024). "It was something I naturally found worked and heard about later": An investigation of body doubling with neurodivergent participants. *Proceedings of the ACM on Human-Computer Interaction.* https://doi.org/10.1145/3689648

Hopkins, L. (2026). *Harder than it should be: Why everything is more exhausting than it used to be and what your brain needs you to know about it.* degrees138.

Hopkins, L. (2026). *It's the circumstances: A psychologist's contrarian guide to depression, systems, and why your brain might be fine.* degrees138.

Siegel, D. J. (2012). *The developing mind: How relationships and the brain interact to shape who we are* (2nd ed.). Guilford Press.

Thomas Craig, K. J., Khan, R., Hariharaputran, S., Gao, J., & Haber, M. (2025). Real-world evaluation of prevalence, cohort characteristics, and healthcare utilization and expenditures among adults and children with autism spectrum disorder, attention-deficit hyperactivity disorder, or both. *BMC Health Services Research, 25,* 1048. https://doi.org/10.1186/s12913-025-13296-2

Chapter 5

Sensory management and environmental design

The café I'm drafting this chapter in has a ceiling fan that wobbles. Not dangerously. Not even visibly, unless you're the kind of person who notices that sort of thing, which, if you're reading this book, you almost certainly are. The wobble produces a rhythmic irregularity in the airflow that my skin registers as a pattern with a flaw in it, and my autistic brain has been tracking the flaw for the past forty minutes while my ADHD brain has been using the ambient noise of the café as regulatory white noise to sustain focus on the paragraph you're now reading.

Both of these things are happening simultaneously. Neither interferes with the other. The wobble tracking runs in the background like a process I can't close. The white noise runs in the foreground like a tool I've learned to use. This is what sensory processing looks like in an AuDHD brain: not a single sensitivity dial turned too high but a mixing desk with forty channels, each set at a different level, several of which you didn't know existed until someone pointed out that most people can't hear the electrical frequency of fluorescent lighting.

Chapter 2 described the sensory paradox of AuDHD—the simultaneous seeking and avoiding, the craving for stimulation that coexists with intolerance for the wrong kind of stimulation. This chapter is about what to do with that paradox. Not how to fix your sensory system, because there's nothing wrong with it. How to arrange the world so that your sensory system can stop working quite so hard to survive it.

THE WORLD GOT LOUDER WHILE YOU WERE AT HOME

The pandemic changed the sensory landscape of daily life in ways that most AuDHD people felt immediately and the neurotypical world is only beginning to acknowledge. For two years, many of us worked from environments we controlled. The lighting was ours. The sound was ours. The temperature, the seating, the presence or absence of other humans—all adjustable. We didn't have language for it at the time, but what we had was an accidental sensory accommodation the scale of which the neurodivergent community had never experienced.

Then the offices reopened, and the accommodation evaporated.

Return-to-office mandates hit AuDHD employees with particular force because the contrast was so stark. You can't un-know what it felt like to work in an environment calibrated to your nervous system. Going back to open-plan offices—the fluorescent lighting, the involuntary social monitoring, the acoustic chaos of thirty people on different phone calls in a room designed by someone who apparently believed that proximity equals collaboration—was not a return to normal. It was a return to a sensory environment whose cost you'd been paying without realising it until you stopped.

The hybrid model that many workplaces have adopted since is, in principle, an improvement. In practice, it's created a new problem: the sensory unpredictability of not knowing, on any given day, how many people will be in the office, which desks will be occupied, whether the meeting you prepared for will be in-person or virtual, and whether the colleague who microwaves fish for lunch will be present. For an autistic brain that manages sensory load through predictability, the hybrid office is arguably worse than the fully open one, because at least the fully open one was consistently terrible.

DESIGNING ENVIRONMENTS RATHER THAN COPING WITH THEM

The most important shift in how I think about sensory management came from a reframe so simple it's almost embarrassing: stop managing your response to the environment and start managing the environment.

This sounds obvious. It isn't, because the entire clinical and self-help apparatus around neurodivergent sensory experience is built on the assumption that you will adapt to the world rather than arranging the world to suit your neurology. Sensory 'strategies' in most of the literature are strategies for tolerating environments that are hostile to your nervous system. Deep breathing. Grounding exercises. Sensory breaks. These are useful in the way that painkillers are useful: they manage the symptom while leaving the cause untouched.

Environmental design is different. It asks: what would this space need to look like for my nervous system to operate without spending resources on sensory defence? The answer is specific to you, because AuDHD sensory profiles are as individual as fingerprints. But the principles are consistent.

Lighting matters more than most people realise. Fluorescent lighting operates at a frequency that many AuDHD brains perceive as flickering even when neurotypical brains register it as steady. The flicker consumes processing resources below conscious awareness, contributing to the 'I'm exhausted and I don't know why' experience that is the background radiation of many AuDHD workdays. Replacing fluorescent with warm LED lighting, using desk lamps instead of overhead lights, or positioning your workspace near a window where natural light is available, is not a luxury. It is removing an invisible tax on your cognitive processing.

Sound is the other major environmental variable. AuDHD auditory processing frequently involves difficulty filtering relevant from irrelevant sound—the cocktail party problem, except it's not a party and you're not having fun. Noise-cancelling headphones are the single most cost-effective sensory accommodation available. I own three pairs: one for the office, one for travel, and a spare for the inevitable day I lose one of the first two, which happens with the frequency you'd expect from someone who lost their reading glasses three times in a single chapter. They don't eliminate sound. They reduce it to a level my auditory processing can manage without consuming the executive function I need for actual work.

Temperature, seating, clothing texture, screen brightness, the distance between you and the nearest source of unpredictable human movement—all of these are design variables, not fixed conditions. The degree to which you can modify them depends on your circumstances. If you work from home, the design is entirely yours. If you work in an office, you may need to negotiate accommodations, which requires disclosure of your neurodivergence, which is a cost-benefit calculation the next chapter on relationships and social connections will address. If you live in shared accommodation, the negotiation is more complex but the principle is the same: every sensory modification that reduces the ambient processing load is an investment in the cognitive resources you need for everything else.

THE SENSE YOU DIDN'T KNOW YOU HAD

There are not five senses. There are at least eight, and the one that matters most for AuDHD daily functioning is the one almost nobody talks about.

Interoception is the ability to sense the internal states of your body: hunger, thirst, temperature, pain, heart rate, the need to use the bathroom, and—critically—emotional states, which are experienced first as bodily sensations before they become nameable feelings. It is, in effect, the body's internal monitoring system, and in AuDHD, it frequently operates with the reliability of a smoke alarm that either doesn't go off when the house is on fire or sounds the alarm when someone makes toast.

A 2025 systematic review and meta-analysis of 31 studies found that interoceptive processing in autistic people is complex and inconsistent rather than simply impaired (Klein et al., 2025). Some autistic people show heightened awareness of internal signals but difficulty interpreting them. Others show reduced awareness altogether.

ADHD adds a further complication: a constantly busy or distracted mind may simply not notice the quiet, steady signals that interoception produces, the way you might not notice a text message arriving during a phone call. The combination in AuDHD means you may be simultaneously over-aware of some bodily signals and completely oblivious to others.

This connects directly to Chapter 3's allostatic load argument. If your interoceptive system doesn't reliably signal hunger, you forget to eat. If it doesn't reliably signal fatigue, you push past the point where your body has the resources to continue. If it doesn't reliably signal emotional overwhelm, you don't recognise the meltdown building until it arrives fully formed, and everyone around you—including you—is startled by an emotional response that appears to come from nowhere but has actually been accumulating all day.

I wrote about this in *The Body Remembers the Fire*. The collapse that chapter documents was not sudden. It was the culmination of months of interoceptive signals I didn't detect: the headache I normalised, the fatigue I attributed to age, the body pain I assumed was orthopaedic rather than fascial. My interoceptive system was sending messages. I wasn't receiving them. Or more precisely, I was receiving them and filing them under 'probably nothing' because I'd spent sixty-six years developing a relationship with my body in which its signals were treated as unreliable narrators rather than accurate reporters.

The practical implication is that AuDHD sensory management needs to include internal senses, not just external ones. Set timers for meals, water, and rest breaks—not because you're incapable of self-care but because your interoceptive system may not alert you to the need at the point when intervention would be most effective. The timers from Chapter 4 are doing double duty: they're executive function prosthetics and interoceptive prosthetics simultaneously.

THE SENSORY BUDGET

I find it useful to think of sensory tolerance as a daily budget. You wake up with a certain amount of sensory capital. Every demand on your sensory processing system—the commute, the office lighting, the meeting, the grocery shop, the social interaction, the unexpected phone call—withdraws from the budget. Rest, solitude, controlled sensory input, and environmental predictability deposit back into it. If you spend more than you earn, you go into sensory debt, and sensory debt accrues interest: the overdrawn system becomes more sensitive, not less, meaning tomorrow's budget starts smaller than today's.

This is why AuDHD people can tolerate something on Monday that destroys them on Friday. The stimulus hasn't changed. The budget has. Understanding your sensory budget—learning to track not just what drains it but at what rate, and what replenishes it most efficiently—is one of the most practically useful forms of self-knowledge an AuDHD person can develop.

The budget metaphor also explains something that bewilders many neurotypical partners, colleagues, and clinicians: the AuDHD person who appears 'fine' all day and then melts down over something trivial in the evening. They're not overreacting to the trivial thing. The trivial thing was the last withdrawal from a budget that was already at zero. The meltdown is the overdraft fee. If you only see the fee, you misunderstand the economics.

. . .

I'm still in the café. The fan is still wobbling. My noise-cancelling headphones are playing brown noise at a volume calibrated to mask the espresso machine without masking the ambient human presence I need for body doubling. I've eaten because my 1pm timer told me to.

I'm sitting with my back to the wall because facing unpredictable movement from behind is a sensory cost I learned to avoid approximately thirty years before I had the vocabulary to explain why. And my military training drummed into me the life-risk of having people enter the room quietly and unseen—'backs to the wall' was not a euphemism.

None of these accommodations is dramatic. All of them are deliberate. Together, they constitute an environment designed for my neurology rather than against it, assembled from available materials in a Vietnamese café that has no idea it's functioning as a therapeutic intervention.

The next chapter covers emotional regulation, mental health, and the body—the territory where sensory experience meets emotional experience, where the internal signals described in the interoception section connect to the feelings they produce, and where the question of what counts as 'dysregulation' gets considerably more interesting when you stop assuming that the neurotypical emotional range is the correct one.

REFERENCES

Hopkins, L. (2026). *The Body Remembers the Fire*. degrees138.

Klein, M., Witthöft, M., & Jungmann, S. M. (2025). Interoception in individuals with autism spectrum disorder: A systematic literature review and meta-analysis. *Frontiers in Psychiatry, 16*, 1573263. https://doi.org/10.3389/fpsyt.2025.1573263

Loureiro, F., Ringold, S. M., & Aziz-Zadeh, L. (2024). Interoception in autism: A narrative review of behavioral and neurobiological data. *Psychology Research and Behavior Management, 17*, 1841–1853. https://doi.org/10.2147/PRBM.S410605

Mahler, K. (2017). *Interoception: The eighth sensory system.* AAPC Publishing.

Siegel, D. J. (2012). *The developing mind: How relationships and the brain interact to shape who we are* (2nd ed.). Guilford Press.

Chapter 6

Emotional regulation, mental health, and the body

Hương asked me why I was angry and I said I wasn't angry. She said my face looked angry. I said my face was doing its own thing and I'd have a word with it later. She gave me the look she gives me when I'm being technically accurate but humanly useless, which is a look I receive with some frequency.

I wasn't angry. I was having an emotion I couldn't identify. It had arrived approximately ninety minutes earlier, somewhere between the second café sua đá and a paragraph about dopaminergic pathways, and it was sitting in my chest like a parcel that had been delivered to the wrong address. I knew it was there. I didn't know what it was. I wouldn't know what it was until approximately 3am, when I'd wake up and think, 'Oh. That was grief. About something that happened in 2014.'

This is AuDHD emotional processing. The feelings are real, intense, and frequently late to identify themselves, like party guests who arrive in costume and refuse to give their names until the host has already spent the evening guessing wrong.

WHAT IF THE FEELINGS ARE RIGHT

Most clinical literature on AuDHD emotional experience uses the word 'dysregulation.' Emotional dysregulation. Affect dysregulation. The implication is that there is a correct way to regulate emotions and your system is failing to do it. I spent forty years in a psychiatric system that treated my emotional responses as symptoms to be managed—as I documented in *Misdiagnosed*—and I have become, understandably I think, suspicious of any framework that begins with the assumption that the neurodivergent emotional response is the wrong one.

In *It's the circumstances*, I made the argument that depression is often an accurate response to genuinely depressing circumstances, and that treating the response as the problem while leaving the circumstances intact is a category error with real clinical consequences. The same argument applies here. If an AuDHD person feels overwhelmed by a sensory environment that is genuinely overwhelming, the overwhelm is not dysregulation. It is regulation working correctly in hostile conditions. If an AuDHD person experiences intense distress after a social interaction that required two hours of continuous masking, the distress is not disproportionate. It is proportionate to a cognitive demand that nobody measured because the diagnostic system doesn't have a unit of measurement for masking cost.

I wonder whether some of what the clinical literature calls emotional dysregulation in AuDHD is actually emotional accuracy—a nervous system responding with appropriate intensity to circumstances that are genuinely as difficult as the response suggests, in a culture that has normalised those circumstances and pathologised the response.

This is not to say that emotional regulation challenges don't exist in AuDHD. They do. But the conversation needs to start with an honest assessment of whether the emotion is the problem or whether the circumstances producing the emotion are the problem, and that assessment rarely happens in a clinical setting where the appointment is fifty minutes and the referral question is 'help this person manage their feelings.'

HOW AUDHD EMOTIONS ACTUALLY WORK

AuDHD emotional processing combines two patterns that interact in ways neither condition's literature fully captures.

Autistic emotional processing is deep but slow. The feeling arrives, settles in the body, and may take hours or days to become legible. You know something is happening. You can feel it physically—the chest tightness, the jaw clenching, the particular quality of exhaustion that is emotional rather than physical. But you can't name it yet. The experience of having a feeling you can't identify is called alexithymia, and approximately 50% of autistic adults experience it to a significant degree (Klein et al., 2025).

ADHD emotional processing is fast and intense. The feeling arrives, fills the room, demands immediate attention, and may be gone by the time you've worked out what it was. The emotional volume knob is set higher than the neurotypical default, and the braking system that would normally modulate the intensity is slower to engage.

AuDHD combines both. You experience emotions with ADHD intensity and autistic processing lag, which means you are flooded by a feeling you can't identify, can't regulate, can't articulate, and may not fully understand until much later—when you're doing something entirely unrelated and the interpretation arrives like a letter that was posted three days ago. My 3am grief revelation is textbook AuDHD emotional processing: the ADHD system registered the emotion in real time with full intensity, the autistic system took eleven years to file it correctly, and my conscious mind received the memo at the worst possible hour.

REJECTION SENSITIVITY AND THE PAIN NOBODY CAN SEE

Rejection sensitive dysphoria—RSD—deserves its own section because it is one of the most common, most painful, and least understood features of the AuDHD emotional landscape.

The term describes the intense, often overwhelming emotional response to perceived rejection or criticism. Perceived is the operative word. The rejection doesn't need to be real. It needs to be processed as real by a nervous system that is simultaneously hyper-alert to social threat (the autistic monitoring system, running continuous surveillance on every interaction for signs of exclusion) and emotionally hair-trigger (the ADHD intensity, which means the response to perceived rejection arrives at full volume with no warm-up period).

A colleague's ambiguous email. A friend's delayed response to a message. A partner's facial expression that might mean disapproval or might mean they're thinking about what to have for lunch. Any of these can trigger an emotional cascade that feels catastrophic—genuinely, physically painful, not metaphorically painful. The pain is as real as a burn. It's just not visible, which means it is routinely dismissed by people who can't see it and misdiagnosed by clinicians who interpret it as anxiety, borderline personality disorder, or melodrama.

The clinical literature on RSD is maturing. What was once dismissed as hypersensitivity is increasingly understood as a neurological phenomenon related to dopaminergic function—the same neurotransmitter system implicated in both ADHD attention regulation and the reward-processing circuits that give social acceptance its emotional valence. RSD is not a character flaw. It is what happens when the brain's social-threat detection system runs at a sensitivity level that was designed for environments considerably more dangerous than a modern office, combined with an emotional braking system that takes longer to engage than the feeling takes to arrive.

ANGER AND THE NEUROLOGICAL EXPLOSION

Jan De Kesel, writing at Thinking-time on Substack, put it with the directness the topic requires: 'Why your brain explodes, and why it's not a character flaw.'

AuDHD anger is a subject most clinical writing handles badly, because the clinical frame for anger is moral rather than neurological. Anger is treated as something to be managed, controlled, de-escalated—the implication being that the anger is excessive and the person producing it should produce less of it. For AuDHD men in particular, who are already subject to cultural expectations about emotional containment, this framing is doubly unhelpful: it pathologises the anger without examining what produced it, and it demands suppression as the price of social acceptability, which is another form of masking, which is another contribution to the allostatic load described in Chapter 3.

What I've observed clinically and experienced personally is that AuDHD anger is frequently the last stage of a processing sequence that went undetected at every earlier stage. The frustration built. The sensory load accumulated. The executive function demands exceeded capacity. The emotional regulation resources—already depleted by the day's masking, translating, and compensating—ran out. And the anger arrived as the system's emergency pressure valve, not as a first response but as a last resort.

Understanding this changes the intervention completely. If anger is the problem, the solution is anger management. If anger is the system's final response to accumulated overload, the solution is reducing the overload—which is what Chapters 4 and 5 were about. The executive function tools and sensory management strategies from those chapters are not separate from emotional regulation. They are emotional regulation, operating upstream.

WHEN THE BODY IS PART OF THE EMOTIONAL PROBLEM

There is an emerging connection between neurodivergent emotional experience and the immune system that the clinical mainstream has barely begun to acknowledge.

Mast cell activation syndrome—MCAS—is a condition in which mast cells, part of the immune system, release excessive inflammatory mediators inappropriately. It produces a bewildering constellation of symptoms including fatigue, brain fog, headaches, gastrointestinal distress, and skin reactions. It is common, rarely diagnosed, and increasingly associated with both neurodivergent conditions and connective tissue disorders like hypermobile Ehlers-Danlos syndrome (hEDS).

A 2025 study by Weinstock and colleagues in *Brain, Behavior, and Immunity—Health* surveyed 553 MCAS patients and 558 controls and found dramatically elevated rates of neuropsychiatric conditions in the MCAS group (Weinstock et al., 2025). Female MCAS patients showed significantly higher rates of ADHD, OCD, bipolar disorder, PTSD, suicidality, anxiety, and depression compared to controls. The odds ratios were striking—and critically, many patients reported symptom improvement after mast-cell-directed treatment, including antihistamines.

Read that again. Psychiatric symptoms improving after antihistamine treatment.

The implications are uncomfortable for a field that has been treating these symptoms as primarily psychological. If immune dysregulation is producing or amplifying the emotional intensity, the sensory sensitivity, the fatigue, and the cognitive fog that AuDHD people experience, then treating the emotional symptoms without investigating the immune system is like mopping the floor while the tap is running. The emerging MCAS-hEDS-neurodivergence connection suggests that for some AuDHD people, what looks like emotional dysregulation may be, in part, an inflammatory process. This doesn't mean everyone with AuDHD has MCAS. It means the question should be asked, and it almost never is.

THE INTEROCEPTIVE GAP

Chapter 5 introduced interoception—the body's internal sensing system. The connection to emotional regulation is direct. Emotions are experienced first as bodily sensations before they become nameable feelings. If your interoceptive system doesn't reliably transmit those early signals, the emotion arrives fully formed without the graduated warning that would normally allow you to regulate it. This is what happened in the collapse I described in *The Body Remembers the Fire*: months of interoceptive signals went undetected—the headache normalised, the fatigue attributed to age, the body pain filed under 'probably nothing'—until the system exceeded its load-bearing capacity and the emergency arrived without a warm-up act.

The practical implication is that improving interoceptive awareness—learning to notice the body's early signals rather than the late ones—is an emotional regulation intervention. The timers from Chapter 4, the sensory budgeting from Chapter 5, the environmental design that reduces ambient overload—all of these reduce the chance that your body's distress signals will be drowned out by the noise of daily functioning until they arrive as a meltdown, a shutdown, or a 3am revelation about grief you didn't know you were carrying.

I'm going to resist the temptation to end this chapter with advice about how to manage AuDHD emotions better, because the whole argument of the chapter has been that managing the emotions is the wrong starting point. The question is not 'how do I regulate my feelings?' The question is: are the circumstances producing those feelings as reasonable as my feelings say they are? And if so, which needs changing—my emotional response, or the circumstances?

The next chapter moves from the internal world to the external one: education and academic success, where the AuDHD brain meets institutional structures that were designed by people who have never, as far as I can tell, met a neurodivergent child. The emotional regulation challenges described here don't stay at home. They walk through the school gates every morning, and what happens next is the subject of Chapter 7.

REFERENCES

Hopkins, L. (2025). *The Body Remembers the Fire*. degrees138.

Hopkins, L. (2025). *It's the circumstances: A psychologist's contrarian guide to depression, systems, and why your brain might be fine*. degrees138.

Hopkins, L. (2025). *Misdiagnosed: When psychiatry mistakes neurodivergence for mental illness*. degrees138.

Klein, M., Witthöft, M., & Jungmann, S. M. (2025). Interoception in individuals with autism spectrum disorder: A systematic literature review and meta-analysis. *Frontiers in Psychiatry, 16*, 1573263. https://doi.org/10.3389/fpsyt.2025.1573263

Weinstock, L. B., Afrin, L. B., Reiersen, A. M., Brook, J., Blitshteyn, S., Ehrlich, G., Schofield, J. R., Kinsella, L., Kaufman, D., Dempsey, T., & Molderings, G. J. (2025). Prevalence and treatment response of neuropsychiatric disorders in mast cell activation syndrome. *Brain, Behavior, & Immunity—Health, 48*, 101048. https://doi.org/10.1016/j.bbih.2025.101048

Chapter 7

Education and academic success

I am currently completing a Master's in Creative Writing at Tabor College, Adelaide. I am sixty-seven years old. My capstone project is a novella co-written with an AI, which I suspect makes me simultaneously the oldest and the most technologically adventurous student in the programme. The irony of an AuDHD man who failed repeatedly within educational systems for four decades finally thriving in one at retirement age is not lost on me, though the university seems unsure whether I'm an inspiring story or an administrative anomaly.

I mention this because the conventional narrative about neurodivergent education is a childhood story: early identification, school accommodations, parental advocacy, transition planning. That narrative matters. But it excludes the substantial population of AuDHD adults who are in education right now—returning to university, completing qualifications they couldn't finish at twenty, pursuing learning for the sheer dopamine-fuelled joy of it—and the even larger population of AuDHD adults whose relationship with formal education was so comprehensively damaged in childhood that they've never gone back.

This chapter is for all of you. The children currently navigating systems designed by people who appear never to have met a neurodivergent student. The parents advocating for those children with the exhausted persistence of someone filing their fourteenth accommodation request this academic year. And the adults wondering whether it's too late to try again, which it isn't, though the system won't make it easy.

THE SPIKY PROFILE AND WHY AVERAGES LIE

The defining cognitive feature of AuDHD in educational settings is the spiky profile—a pattern of abilities that varies so dramatically across domains that no average score can meaningfully represent the person. You might score in the 99th percentile for verbal reasoning and the 5th percentile for processing speed. You might produce postgraduate-level analysis on topics that engage your interest system and primary-school-level output on topics that don't. You might demonstrate extraordinary capacity for sustained, deep learning in one subject and appear unable to retain basic information in another, not because you can't learn but because your brain allocates resources according to a priority system that bears no relationship to the curriculum's priority system.

The spiky profile is neurological, not motivational. This is the single most important thing that educators, parents, and AuDHD students themselves need to understand. The variation between peaks and troughs is not explained by effort, attitude, or interest—though interest certainly amplifies the peaks. It is explained by the uneven development and functioning of the neural architecture supporting different cognitive operations. The brain regions and neurotransmitter systems powering your strengths operate differently from those powering your weaknesses, and no amount of trying harder will make the weak systems perform like the strong ones, for the same reason that no amount of enthusiasm will make a bicycle perform like a motorcycle.

Educational systems are built on the assumption of flat profiles. The curriculum expects relatively consistent performance across subjects. Assessment assumes that if you can demonstrate competence in one context, you can demonstrate it in all contexts. Grading averages your peaks and troughs into a single number that represents neither accurately. An AuDHD student with extraordinary capacity in three subjects and significant impairment in two receives a 'C average' that makes them look mediocre when they are, in fact, simultaneously gifted and disabled—a combination the system has no framework for and no language to describe except 'inconsistent,' which it means as a criticism.

WHAT THE SYSTEM GETS WRONG

The Australian education system operates under the Disability Standards for Education 2005, which are currently being reviewed by the federal government. The Standards require educational institutions to make 'reasonable adjustments' for students with disabilities, which sounds like a robust protection until you discover that the definition of 'reasonable' is determined largely by the institution, that the enforcement mechanism requires the student or their family to lodge a complaint, and that the complaints process is so demanding of time, energy, and executive function that it effectively selects against the people it's supposed to protect. An AuDHD student whose executive function is already at capacity does not have the spare cognitive resources to navigate a bureaucratic complaints process. This is not a design flaw. It is the system functioning exactly as designed, for a population it wasn't designed for.

The Nationally Consistent Collection of Data on School Students with Disability—the NCCD—requires all Australian schools to report annually on students with disability and the adjustments they receive. The NCCD uses four levels of adjustment: support within quality differentiated teaching practice, supplementary, substantial, and extensive. These are real categories with real funding implications, and they have the bureaucratic elegance of a system designed by people who have never had to explain to a sobbing ten-year-old why the classroom lights sound angry. In principle, the NCCD creates accountability.

In practice, the level of adjustment a student receives is determined by the school, documented by the school, and reported by the school, with limited external verification. The incentive structure rewards underreporting, because higher levels of adjustment cost more to provide and the funding model doesn't always cover the gap. Asking a school to honestly report its own failures in supporting disabled students is a bit like asking a restaurant to honestly report its own health code violations: technically required, structurally unlikely, and consequential mainly for the people eating the food.

For AuDHD students specifically, the system's failure is compounded by the masking problem described in Chapter 1. A student who can perform adequately in a structured assessment environment—because their autistic architecture provides the structure and their ADHD architecture provides the performance energy —may not qualify for adjustments that they desperately need in less structured contexts. The assessment captures the peak. The daily reality lives in the troughs. And the gap between the two is invisible to a system that measures competence in controlled conditions and assumes it transfers to uncontrolled ones.

WHAT ACTUALLY HELPS

The accommodations that make the biggest difference for AuDHD students are, with depressing consistency, the simplest and cheapest to implement. Extra time on assessments. The option to sit exams in a separate, low-sensory room. Permission to use noise-cancelling headphones during class. Flexibility in assignment deadlines that accounts for the boom-and-bust energy cycle rather than assuming consistent output across the semester. Access to lecture recordings so that the ADHD brain, which was building a complex mental model of the topic while simultaneously missing three key facts because someone two rows back was clicking a pen, can fill in the gaps later.

The accommodations that make the second-biggest difference are more structural. AuDHD students benefit enormously from having one consistent point of contact within the institution—a disability services coordinator, a trusted teacher, anyone who understands the profile and can translate between the student's needs and the institution's requirements. Without this intermediary, the student must advocate for themselves in every interaction with every staff member, re-explaining their neurology each time, which is the executive-function equivalent of filling out the same form repeatedly for different departments of the same organisation. Which, now I think about it, is literally what it is.

For younger students, the parent advocacy role is critical and exhausting. I've worked with families where one parent has effectively become a full-time unpaid educational advocate, spending hours each week in meetings, writing emails, reviewing Individual Education Plans, and translating between the school's language of compliance and the child's lived experience of not being supported. The emotional toll on these parents is significant, and it is almost entirely invisible to the system they're navigating. If you are one of these parents: I see you. Your exhaustion is real. Your frustration is justified. And the fact that you have to fight this hard for accommodations that should be automatic is a failure of the system, not a failure of your child.

HIGHER EDUCATION AND THE ADULTS WHO COME BACK

University is, paradoxically, often easier for AuDHD adults than school was. The reasons are structural: you choose your subjects, which means the interest system is engaged. The timetable is less rigid. The social demands are optional. Nobody makes you sit in a fluorescent-lit room for six hours with thirty other humans and a clicking pen. The content is deeper, which suits the autistic capacity for sustained focus on a single topic. And if you're returning as a mature student, you bring decades of compensatory strategies, self-knowledge, and sheer bloody-mindedness that eighteen-year-olds haven't had time to develop.

The challenges are real but different. Assignment submission systems have the user-friendliness of a tax return designed by someone who enjoys bureaucracy. Group work assumes that all participants have equivalent social communication skills and that collaboration is inherently beneficial, which are two assumptions that an AuDHD student would like to interrogate in some detail but probably shouldn't during the first tutorial. And the shift to online and hybrid learning, accelerated by the pandemic, has created a sensory and executive-function landscape that nobody has designed for neurodivergent students because nobody asked them.

My own experience at Tabor has been positive, which I attribute to three factors: I chose the programme because the subject engaged my interest system to the point of hyperfocus, I disclosed my AuDHD early and found the staff receptive, and I am old enough and sufficiently past caring about other people's expectations that I do the work on my own terms rather than performing the role of 'good student' as the institution imagines it. That last factor is not an accommodation the institution provides. It's a consequence of being sixty-seven and having run out of the energy required to pretend.

For AuDHD adults considering a return to education: the interest system is your engine. If the subject engages it, you will produce work that surprises everyone, including yourself. If it doesn't, you will produce nothing, and no amount of discipline, motivation, or self-criticism will change that, because discipline is a neurotypical word for a neurotypical capacity that your brain provides on its own terms or not at all. Choose what interests you. Disclose early. Use every accommodation available. And if the institution doesn't understand your neurology, remember that you are not the one with the comprehension problem.

. . .

The universe spent 13.8 billion years evolving a nervous system capable of abstract thought, pattern recognition, creative synthesis, and the extraordinary achievement of feeling stupid in a maths class. AuDHD brains are not broken brains in the wrong school. They are unusual brains in schools designed for the usual ones. The mismatch produces real suffering, real underachievement, and real damage to self-concept that can persist for decades—as I can confirm from personal experience and from the forty years of wrong diagnoses that followed my own school years.

The next chapter covers employment and career development, where the spiky profile meets the labour market and the question becomes: how do you build a working life around a brain that is extraordinary at some things and catastrophically unreliable at others? The answer, it turns out, involves less 'finding the right job' and more 'designing the right conditions,' which is the same argument this entire book has been making from Chapter 1.

REFERENCES

Australian Government Department of Education. (2025). *2025 review of the Disability Standards for Education*. https://www.education.gov.au/disability-standards-education-2005

Doyle, N. (2020). Neurodiversity at work: A biopsychosocial model and the impact on working adults. *British Medical Bulletin, 135*(1), 108–125. https://doi.org/10.1093/bmb/ldaa021

Nationally Consistent Collection of Data on School Students with Disability. (2025). *NCCD guidelines*. https://www.nccd.edu.au

Chapter 8

Employment and career development

I have had, by my count, somewhere between fifteen and twenty jobs. I stopped counting at a point when the number became less a career history and more a cry for help. Social media evangelist. Military serviceman. Counselling psychologist. Author. Courier. Recruitment counsellor. Factory hand. Call centre employee. Photographer. Digital entrepreneur. University lecturer. Disability pensioner.

Each transition made perfect sense from the inside, the interest system engaged, the dopamine flowed, the autistic capacity for deep immersion produced work of genuine quality, and looked, from the outside, like a man who couldn't commit. The HR departments of the world have a word for this pattern. They call it instability. I call it a spiky profile meeting a labour market that rewards the flat one.

Employment is where AuDHD meets economics, and economics is less interested in your neurological architecture than it is in whether you can show up at the same place at the same time and produce consistent output for decades. The AuDHD brain can produce extraordinary output. It cannot produce consistent output. This distinction is the source of approximately 90% of the employment difficulties described in this chapter, and the remaining 10% is open-plan offices.

THE INTERVIEW, OR THE MASK'S AUDITION

The job interview is a masking event. This is so obvious that nobody says it, which is how you know it's important. The interview rewards exactly the skills that AuDHD people find most effortful: spontaneous social performance under time pressure, in an unfamiliar sensory environment, with a stranger who is simultaneously evaluating your competence and your likability, whilst you manage the eye contact, the body language, the vocal modulation, and the executive function demand of answering questions you weren't given in advance about topics the interviewer considers important but your interest system may not.

The AuDHD person who excels in interviews is not demonstrating job fitness. They are demonstrating masking proficiency, which is a different skill entirely and one that tells the employer precisely nothing about whether the person can do the work, in much the same way that an audition tells you whether someone can act but not whether they can live. The person who masks brilliantly in the interview then arrives at the job and discovers that the daily sensory, social, and executive function demands were not visible from the audition room, and the employer discovers that the person who interviewed so impressively doesn't quite match the person who turned up.

The AuDHD person who interviews badly, conversely, may be the best candidate in the pool and will never get the chance to prove it, because the selection system filtered them out at the stage where masking capacity was being measured and job-relevant competence was not. I have lost count of the number of clients I've worked with who are extraordinary at their actual jobs and catastrophically poor at the theatre of getting hired. The standard advice, practise your answers, research the company, arrive early, make eye contact, is the neurotypical equivalent of telling a wheelchair user to practise walking: technically describing the desired outcome whilst comprehensively ignoring the mechanism that prevents it.

THE SYSTEM'S FAVOURITE EXPLANATION FOR EVERYTHING

Lindsey Mack, writing at *The Complexity Edge* on Substack, published a piece in March 2026 that stopped me mid-paragraph with the force of being accurately described by someone who'd never met me. She called it *You Were the System's Favorite Explanation for Everything.* Her argument was that organisations routinely assign roles to neurodivergent people that serve the system rather than the person, and then, when the person burns out, the system treats the burnout as evidence of individual deficiency rather than structural exploitation.

I wrote about this dynamic from the systemic angle in my book, *The Convenient Monster*: the way organisations produce harm while locating the blame in individuals. Mack's contribution is to describe how it feels from the inside of the person being blamed. The AuDHD employee who becomes the 'go-to problem solver' because their pattern recognition and hyperfocus produce results nobody else can match, who takes on more because the dopamine hit of being valued is the most reliable source of workplace motivation available, who compensates for the system's dysfunction because their autistic architecture notices the dysfunction and their ADHD architecture can't resist trying to fix it. Until they can't. At which point the system, having extracted the value, expresses disappointment that the person 'couldn't handle the workload.'

The workload was the system's workload. It got assigned to one person because that person was good at it and didn't have the social skills or the self-preservation instinct to say no. This is not a personal failing. This is a structural dynamic that the neurodiversity hiring conversation needs to confront honestly if it wants to be more than corporate window dressing.

HOW BURNOUT ACTUALLY HAPPENS

The AuDHD employment burnout cycle follows a pattern so predictable that I could set my watch by it, if I could find my watch, which I can't, because executive function. The cycle has four phases, and the phases are invisible to the employer until the fourth one, which is the one that looks like failure and is actually the inevitable conclusion of the three that preceded it.

Phase one: engagement. The interest system locks on. The new role is novel, which means dopamine is available, which means the ADHD brain is functional, which means the autistic capacity for deep work produces output that impresses everyone. The employer sees a star performer. The employee feels, briefly, like a person whose brain works. This phase lasts weeks to months, depending on the complexity of the role and the novelty budget it provides.

Phase two: compensation. The novelty fades. The dopamine supply drops. The tasks that were stimulating become routine, and routine without interest is the ADHD brain's kryptonite. Meanwhile, the sensory and social demands of the workplace continue at their original level, which was manageable when cognitive resources were abundant and becomes expensive when they are not. The employee begins compensating: working harder to produce the same output, masking more intensively to conceal the growing difficulty, spending evenings and weekends recovering from workdays that the employer considers normal and the employee experiences as an endurance event. The employer sees consistent performance. The employee feels the gap widening between what they are producing and what it is costing to produce it.

Phase three: depletion. The compensatory strategies begin consuming more resources than they generate. The allostatic load Chapter 3 described is accumulating in real time: elevated cortisol, disrupted sleep, chronic low-grade inflammation, the body keeping an invoice the employer will never see. Executive function deteriorates. Sensory tolerance shrinks. Masking capacity degrades. The employee starts making mistakes, missing deadlines, withdrawing from social interactions that were previously managed. The employer notices 'a change in performance.' The employee knows the performance hasn't changed. The capacity to sustain it has.

Phase four: collapse. The mask fails. The employee either leaves, is managed out, or has a visible crisis that gets coded as a mental health episode rather than as the predictable conclusion of an unsustainable accommodation deficit. The exit interview, if there is one, documents the individual's failure to maintain performance standards. It does not document the workplace's failure to provide conditions in which the performance was sustainable. The employee adds the experience to their growing collection of jobs that started brilliantly and ended badly, and the collection reinforces the narrative that the problem is them, when the problem was the four-phase cycle that the workplace generated and the employee absorbed.

I have lived this cycle in most of my fifteen to twenty jobs. The duration varies. The outcome does not.

THE PERFORMANCE REVIEW AND THE SPIKY PROFILE

Annual performance reviews are designed for flat profiles. They assume that competence is roughly consistent across domains, that improvement is linear, and that a single rating can meaningfully represent a year's work. For an AuDHD employee whose output is extraordinary in three domains and absent in two, the performance review is a mathematical averaging exercise that produces a number representing a person who does not exist.

The review says, 'meets expectations.' The reality is: exceeds expectations spectacularly in the areas the interest system engages, and fails to meet expectations in the areas it doesn't, and the average of spectacular and failing is a fictional mediocrity that satisfies nobody and describes nobody. The employee knows the rating is wrong. The manager knows the rating is wrong. But the system requires a number, and the number requires an average, and the average requires pretending that the peaks and troughs are symptoms of inconsistency rather than features of the architecture.

The promotion criteria are worse. Most corporate promotion frameworks reward 'leadership presence,' 'stakeholder engagement,' 'strategic communication,' and 'consistent delivery across multiple priorities,' which is a wish list assembled by someone who has never met a neurodivergent person and which functions, in practice, as a masking proficiency assessment conducted annually and rewarded with increased responsibility, which requires increased masking, which consumes increased resources, which accelerates the burnout cycle described above. The promotion pathway for AuDHD employees is a treadmill that speeds up every time you reach for the controls.

NEURODIVERSITY HIRING PROGRAMMES AND THE QUESTION NOBODY ASKS

The rise of neurodiversity hiring programmes at major corporations, SAP, Microsoft, JPMorgan Chase, EY, and others, has been widely reported and generally celebrated. The narrative is appealing: forward-thinking companies discover that neurodivergent employees bring unique strengths, create dedicated hiring pathways, and everybody wins.

The reality is more complicated, and the complication matters. Most neurodiversity hiring programmes recruit for specific technical roles, software testing, data analysis, cybersecurity, where the autistic capacity for sustained attention to detail and pattern recognition produces measurable competitive advantage. These programmes are genuine and many of the people hired through them are doing excellent work in roles that suit their strengths. That's real.

What's less often discussed is that these programmes recruit a narrow slice of the neurodivergent population, typically young, male, technically skilled autistic people with minimal support needs, and the corporate environments they're recruited into are rarely redesigned to accommodate neurodivergent needs beyond the specific accommodations provided to the programme participants.

The neurodivergent employee gets a quiet room and an adjusted interview process. The open-plan office, the mandatory social events, the promotion criteria based on 'leadership presence' and 'stakeholder engagement,' and the performance review system that assumes consistent output across all domains: none of that changes. The company gets to announce a neurodiversity programme in a press release and continue operating an environment that would disable most neurodivergent people within six months.

This is, if you'll forgive the technical terminology, having your cake and eating it while charging the cake for rent.

The question nobody asks is: what happens to these employees in five years? Are they promoted? Are they retained? Do they burn out at the same rate as unaccommodated neurodivergent employees, just with a nicer onboarding experience? The longitudinal data is thin, and the corporate enthusiasm for announcing these programmes significantly outpaces the corporate enthusiasm for publishing outcome data. I wonder whether that gap is accidental.

THE DISCLOSURE CALCULATION

Whether to disclose your AuDHD diagnosis to an employer is the question I'm asked most often by neurodivergent clients navigating the workplace. I wish I could give a simple answer. I can't, because the calculation depends on variables that are specific to your situation, your workplace, your manager, and your country's legal protections, which vary from robust to decorative.

In Australia, the Disability Discrimination Act 1992 prohibits discrimination on the basis of disability, including neurodevelopmental conditions. In practice, proving that a workplace decision was motivated by disclosed neurodivergence is extremely difficult, and the process of pursuing a complaint is so demanding that it functions as its own deterrent. The legal protection is real in theory and unreliable in practice, which is the kind of sentence that should make everyone uncomfortable but surprises nobody who has actually tried to use the system.

The potential benefits of disclosure include access to formal accommodations, legal protection against performance management for disability-related difficulties, and the relief of not having to mask continuously at work. The potential costs include being perceived as less capable, being passed over for promotion, being assigned to a narrower range of responsibilities, and encountering the specific kind of well-meaning condescension that arrives when someone has just attended a two-hour neurodiversity awareness training and now believes they understand your brain better than you do, which has the same relationship to actual understanding that a two-hour wine tasting has to running a vineyard. Both the benefits and the costs are real. The calculation is personal.

What I tell clients is this: disclose to the system only when you need something from the system that you can't get without disclosure. You don't owe your employer your diagnostic history. You owe them the work you agreed to do. If you need accommodations to do that work, disclosure is the mechanism for obtaining them. If you don't, the information is yours to share or not share as you choose.

SELF-EMPLOYMENT AND THE ACCIDENTAL ENTREPRENEUR

A disproportionate number of AuDHD adults end up self-employed, and the reason is structural rather than aspirational. Self-employment solves several of the problems that conventional employment creates: you control your sensory environment, you set your own schedule, you choose what you work on, and nobody requires you to attend a team-building exercise involving trust falls and a ropes course. The interest system drives the work. The autistic capacity for deep expertise creates the value. The ADHD capacity for novelty drives the business development. And the absence of a line manager means nobody is measuring your output on a scale designed for a flat profile.

The challenges are equally structural. Self-employment requires executive function for administration, financial management, and the relentless initiating of tasks that don't trigger the interest system. Invoicing is not interesting. Tax compliance is not interesting. Following up on unpaid invoices is not interesting and is also socially uncomfortable, which is a double penalty for an AuDHD brain. The feast-and-famine income cycle that characterises freelance work maps onto the boom-and-bust energy cycle of AuDHD in ways that can amplify both: you hyperfocus during the boom, overcommit, burn out, and then can't work during the bust, which creates financial stress, which increases allostatic load, which depletes the resources needed to restart.

I run multiple businesses from Đà Lạt. I'm writing this book, maintaining a clinical practice via telehealth, publishing on Substack, and managing several online content brands. This sounds impressively productive until you learn that the administrative scaffolding holding it all together is Hương, a whiteboard, and a rotating cast of digital tools that I use with passionate intensity for approximately three weeks before abandoning them for the next one.

The work gets done. The systems for doing the work change continuously. If you're self-employed and AuDHD, your business model is probably brilliant and your filing system is probably a disaster. Both of these things can be true at the same time, and the sooner you stop feeling guilty about the filing system and start designing around it, the better.

WHAT THE PANDEMIC PROVED

The pandemic forced the largest uncontrolled experiment in workplace accommodation in history. Millions of neurodivergent employees suddenly worked from environments they controlled, on schedules they could adjust, without the sensory assault of open-plan offices or the social performance demands of in-person interaction. Productivity data showed that for many knowledge workers, including neurodivergent ones, output was maintained or improved.

Then the offices reopened, and the return-to-office mandates arrived with the institutional confidence of organisations that had learned nothing. The data said remote work functioned. The management philosophy said presence equalled productivity. The management philosophy won, because management philosophies always win against data when the people making the decisions are the ones who prefer offices.

For AuDHD employees, the hybrid compromise is better than full-time office work and worse than consistent remote work, for reasons Chapter 5 described: the unpredictability of hybrid schedules creates sensory and executive function costs that a consistent arrangement, even a consistently office-based one, would not. The best arrangement, when it's available, is negotiated flexibility, the ability to work from wherever your nervous system functions best, with in-person attendance for specific purposes rather than arbitrary days. Not all employers offer this. Not all roles allow it. But if yours does, it's worth more than almost any other accommodation on the list, because it addresses the environmental mismatch directly rather than applying compensatory strategies to an environment that shouldn't need compensating for.

The career advice industry is built on the assumption that there is a right job for everyone and the task is to find it. For AuDHD people, the more useful assumption is that there are right conditions, and the task is to design them. The right conditions involve an environment that doesn't exhaust your sensory system, a schedule that accommodates your energy cycle, work that engages your interest system, and a degree of autonomy that lets you operate on your own terms rather than performing the role of 'normal employee' as someone else imagined it.

Finding those conditions requires self-knowledge, negotiation, and a willingness to prioritise sustainability over status. It sometimes requires leaving jobs that look good on paper but cost more in allostatic load than they pay in salary. It always requires understanding that the employment difficulties you've experienced are not evidence of your limitations. They are evidence of a labour market designed for a different brain, and the labour market's refusal to redesign itself is not your problem to solve. It is, however, your problem to survive, which is a less satisfying distinction than it should be and one that this chapter cannot resolve but can at least name honestly.

The next chapter is about relationships and social connections, which is where the masks we wear at work come home with us and the question becomes: what happens to love, friendship, and intimacy when you stop performing?

REFERENCES

Doyle, N. (2020). Neurodiversity at work: A biopsychosocial model and the impact on working adults. *British Medical Bulletin, 135*(1), 108–125. https://doi.org/10.1093/bmb/ldaa021

Hopkins, L. (2026). *The Convenient Monster:* Why we blame villains and ignore systems. degrees138.

Mack, L. (2026, March). You were the system's favorite explanation for everything. *The Complexity Edge.* https://thecomplexityedge.substack.com

Chapter 9

Relationships, social connections, and the different minds that find each other

You're at a party. You've been performing 'relaxed and socially engaged' for approximately ninety minutes, which has consumed more cognitive resources than most people spend on a full day at the office. You've laughed at the right moments, maintained appropriate eye contact, navigated three conversations about topics you have no interest in, and successfully suppressed the observation that the host's playlist has been alternating between two tempo ranges in a pattern that is almost certainly unintentional but is now the only thing your autistic brain can hear. You are, by every visible measure, having a lovely time.

Then you notice someone across the room who is also, very clearly, not having a lovely time while appearing to have one. You recognise the mask because you're wearing the same one. The performance is flawless. The exhaustion underneath it is visible only to someone running the same software. You make eye contact. Something happens that the clinical literature hasn't named yet but that the neurodivergent community calls recognition: the experience of encountering a brain that speaks the same language as yours, in a room full of people speaking a language you've learned but will never think in.

This chapter is about what happens next. About the relationships that form between different minds. About what happens when the mask comes off and the relationships built around the masked self discover they were built around someone who doesn't exist anymore. And about what it looks like to build connection from scratch when the performance of connection is the only version you were ever taught.

THE DIFFERENT MINDS THAT FIND EACH OTHER

Neurodivergent people find each other with a frequency that statistical chance can't fully explain. AuDHD adults disproportionately form romantic partnerships, close friendships, and professional collaborations with other neurodivergent people—often before either party has been diagnosed. The attraction is not to the diagnosis. It's to the quality of interaction: the depth rather than breadth of conversation, the tolerance for intensity, the shared understanding that silence can be comfortable rather than hostile, the mutual recognition that 'normal' social pacing feels performative from the inside.

I call this neurocomplex attraction, and I've moved it from an appendix in the third edition of this book to the main chapter because it deserves to be here. It names something AuDHD people experience constantly and rarely see validated: the gravitational pull toward minds that operate at similar frequencies. It explains why your closest friendships probably feel effortless in a way that your 'normal' social interactions never do. It explains why your romantic history may include a disproportionate number of partners who turned out to be neurodivergent, diagnosed or not. And it explains the particular grief of relationships with neurotypical people who genuinely love you but will never quite understand the internal experience you're describing, because they don't have the reference architecture.

The neurocomplex attraction pattern also explains something that the relationship literature handles badly: the AuDHD tendency to seek intensity as a proxy for connection. When ordinary intimacy—the quiet, low-stimulation experience of simply existing alongside another person—was never modelled by your social learning, because your social learning was all performance and no rest, intensity becomes the signal for 'this is real.' The deep conversation at 2am. The hyperfocus on a new relationship. The emotional merging that happens when two neurodivergent brains lock onto each other and forget that the rest of the world exists. It feels like connection because it is stimulating, and stimulation is what your dopamine system recognises as engagement. The problem is that intensity is not the same as intimacy, and the relationships built primarily on intensity tend to burn at a temperature that is unsustainable—exhilarating at first, exhausting by month six, and catastrophic by year two.

Real connection, the kind that sustains, is quieter than that. Learning the difference is one of the most important and most difficult things an AuDHD person can do.

When two AuDHD people partner, the neurocomplex attraction is doubled—and so is the risk. The mutual understanding is genuine: neither partner needs to explain why the supermarket is exhausting, why plans change without warning, or why 3am is a productive work hour. The shared neurology creates a sense of being finally seen that can feel, after decades of performing for neurotypical partners, like coming home. But two dysregulated nervous systems under the same roof also means two people whose executive function fails at the same time, whose sensory overload triggers compound rather than balance, and whose ADHD impulsivity meets no autistic brake because the other person's brake is also offline. The best AuDHD partnerships I've observed—clinically and personally—are the ones where both people understand that mutual recognition is the foundation, not the whole house. You still need to build the rooms.

A RELATIONSHIP THAT WORKS AND WHY

Hương is not neurodivergent. Our relationship works not because she understands my AuDHD from the inside but because she pays attention to what it does from the outside and adjusts without requiring me to explain the mechanism every time. She texts the dinner plan instead of asking in the moment. She reads the room when I can't read myself. She recognises the particular quality of silence that means 'processing' rather than 'angry,' and she doesn't fill it with questions. She tolerates the hyperfocus without taking it personally, even when the hyperfocus is on a paragraph about allostatic load at 7pm and the dinner she made is going cold in the kitchen.

This is not neurocomplex attraction. This is something arguably rarer: a neurotypical person who accommodates a neurodivergent partner through observation and care rather than shared neurology. It works because she treats my needs as information rather than inconvenience. The distinction matters. Many neurotypical partners interpret AuDHD needs as criticism—'you need quiet' becomes 'you think I'm too loud,' 'you need advance warning about plans' becomes 'you think I'm disorganised.' Hương skipped that interpretation somewhere early on, probably around the point where she realised that my sensory needs had nothing to do with her and everything to do with a nervous system running specifications she hadn't been given a manual for. Neither had I, but at least I was living inside the hardware.

I tell you this not as a relationship recommendation—'find a Vietnamese woman who brings food without asking' is not clinical advice, however tempting it might be as a lifestyle suggestion—but as evidence that AuDHD relationships can work across neurotypes when the neurotypical partner is willing to observe, accommodate, and resist the urge to interpret everything through their own processing framework. The accommodation is not one-directional. I have learned things from Hương about social timing, emotional expression, and the Vietnamese concept of tình cảm—the deep feeling-bond between people—that my autistic brain would never have developed independently. The exchange is genuine. It just operates in a different currency than most relationship advice assumes.

WHAT MASKING BUILT AND WHAT IT COST

Lindsey Mack, writing at *The Complexity Edge* on Substack, published a piece that I think is one of the best things written about neurodivergent social experience. She called it *You Stopped Masking and Accidentally Lost Your Social Life*, and it names a grief that doesn't have a clinical term yet: the grief of looking up one day and realising that the people who knew you best never actually knew you at all.

Her central insight is devastating in its precision: masking builds a skill adjacent to friendship but not friendship. The masked self was genuinely good at connection. People liked that person. Some of them loved him. The friendships worked, by external measures, for a long time. But the performance consumed exactly the resources that would have been needed to build actual intimacy. The masked self was so busy reading the room, calibrating responses, managing impressions, and performing ease that there was never a moment of just existing next to someone without it meaning something or going somewhere.

That's not a description of social awkwardness. That's a description of a particular kind of loneliness that looks, from the outside, like a rich social life. I had that social life. I had the dinner parties and the professional network and the people who said 'we should catch up more often' with every indication of sincerity. And when the mask started slipping after my diagnosis—when I began saying 'actually, I find this restaurant unbearably loud' instead of smiling through the sensory assault—some of those relationships revealed that they had been built on a foundation of my performance rather than my presence. The performance had been very good. The person underneath it was someone they hadn't met.

WHERE YOU ARE AFTER THE MASK COMES OFF

Mack identifies four positions that AuDHD adults occupy after unmasking, and most of us recognise more than one. I recognised three.

The Drifter. Friendships that haven't ended dramatically but have gone quiet in a way that feels permanent. The calls that stopped coming. The invitations that thinned out. The mutual fade that has no fight to point to and therefore no resolution to seek. You can't grieve a friendship that didn't end; it just became so quiet that you eventually stopped listening for it. The Drifter position is the most common and the most confusing, because there's nobody to be angry at and nothing to repair. The friendship was built on a version of you that no longer exists, and neither of you knows how to renegotiate the terms.

The Revealer. You unmasked, and the friendship buckled under the new shape. You told someone the truth about your sensory needs, or your social limits, or the fact that the thing they thought was spontaneity was actually a carefully managed performance, and they couldn't hold it. Not because they were cruel but because the person they'd befriended was the mask, and the face underneath it was a stranger. The Revealer grieves the relationship and the rejection simultaneously, and the rejection feels like confirmation of the fear that drove the masking in the first place: that the real you is not someone people want to be around.

The Performer in Recovery. Still showing up as the masked version in some relationships because the cost of dropping it feels higher than the cost of maintaining it. You know the performance is unsustainable. You can feel the allostatic load of it now, in a way you couldn't before diagnosis. But the friendships are real, the people matter, and the prospect of losing them by being honest is more frightening than the certainty of exhaustion from continuing to pretend. This position is the most psychologically expensive, because you're paying the masking cost with full awareness of the price.

The person Starting From Zero. No close friends. Building from nothing. This is the position I've seen most often in my clinical work with late-diagnosed adults. They arrive with a social architecture that was constructed entirely by the mask, and when the mask comes off, there's nothing underneath it—not because they're incapable of connection but because the mask consumed the resources that connection requires. Starting from zero at forty, or fifty, or sixty-six, is a particular kind of courage that the self-help literature rarely acknowledges because the self-help literature assumes you have a social foundation to work from.

What unites all four positions is an ambiguous grief—the kind that has no funeral, no clean break, no socially recognised loss to point to and say 'this is what I'm mourning.' You are grieving a version of yourself that was never real and the relationships that version maintained. You are grieving the years spent performing connection instead of experiencing it. And you are grieving the discovery that some of the people you loved most loved a character you played rather than the person who played it. This grief doesn't appear in the bereavement literature because nobody died. But something ended, and the ending is real even if nobody else noticed it happening.

REBUILDING AFTER THE MASK COMES OFF

Mack's practical architecture for rebuilding is the most useful framework I've encountered, and I've read a lot of frameworks. It works because it starts from where AuDHD people actually are rather than where the social skills literature thinks they should be.

Start smaller than feels meaningful. The instinct when you've identified a pattern this significant is to address it at scale—to have the big honest conversation, the dramatic reveal, the moment of truth. That instinct is almost always wrong. Big conversations require big executive function, big emotional regulation, and big social stamina, all of which are depleted resources in someone who has just stopped masking. Start with one text. One honest answer to 'how are you?' One moment of not performing. The AuDHD brain wants to solve the entire social architecture at once because the ADHD side sees the full picture and wants to fix it immediately while the autistic side has identified the system failure and wants to redesign the entire system from scratch. Both impulses are understandable. Both will exhaust you before you've started.

Practice the incomplete reveal. Masking trains a binary: full mask or full disclosure. The unmasked AuDHD adult often swings between performing normality and dumping their entire diagnostic history on someone who asked how their weekend was. The incomplete reveal is one true thing at a time. 'I'm finding this restaurant quite loud' rather than a twenty-minute lecture on sensory processing disorder. 'I need to leave early tonight' rather than a detailed explanation of your allostatic load budget. The incomplete reveal builds trust incrementally, which is how trust is actually built, despite what the movies suggest about the redemptive power of the grand confession.

Let the boring be the point. This is the one that changes everything, and it is the hardest for an AuDHD brain to learn. Real intimacy lives in the going-nowhere moments—watching television, cooking dinner, sitting in comfortable silence—and masked people have been waiting for the going-somewhere ones. AuDHD people often seek intensity as a proxy for connection because the ordinary intimacy of just existing alongside someone was never modelled by the masked social life, which was always performing, always going somewhere, always on. Learning to tolerate ordinariness without reaching for stimulation is, for an AuDHD brain, a genuinely difficult skill. The ADHD architecture is screaming for novelty. The autistic architecture is screaming for meaning. And ordinary human companionship provides neither on demand, which is why it took me sixty-seven years to discover that the best part of my relationship with Hương is dinner on a Wednesday at our favourite noodles place when nothing happens and we don't talk about anything important and the silence between us is the kind that means everything is fine rather than the kind that means someone is performing fineness.

Repair out loud and quickly when the old pattern wins. You will mask again. The performance is decades old and it doesn't uninstall cleanly. When you catch yourself performing, name it: 'I just did the thing where I pretend everything's fine. It isn't. Can I try that again?' The repair matters more than the lapse. Relationships that can tolerate repair are relationships that can hold the real person. Relationships that require perfection are relationships that require the mask, and we already know what the mask costs.

Receive without deflecting. This is the one Mack identifies that I find hardest, and I suspect many AuDHD readers will recognise the difficulty. When someone offers kindness, compliment, or help, the masked reflex is to deflect: 'oh, it's nothing,' 'you don't have to do that,' 'I'm fine.' The deflection is masking in miniature—performing self-sufficiency to avoid the vulnerability of being seen as someone who needs things. Receiving without deflecting is an act of trust. It says: I will let you see that I need this, and I will trust you not to use that knowledge against me. For someone whose social learning was built on the premise that needs are liabilities, this is radical.

WHAT THE NERVOUS SYSTEM DOES TO LOVE

Barbara Lazarony, a licensed therapist writing at *Love on the Autism Spectrum* on Substack, focuses on the nervous system dynamics that shape neurodivergent relationships. Her work names patterns that most couples therapists don't recognise because most couples therapy was developed for neurotypical nervous systems.

The flight response disguised as busyness is one I've seen in nearly every AuDHD relationship I've worked with, including my own. When emotional proximity becomes overwhelming—not because you don't love the person but because your nervous system has run out of capacity to process one more input—the AuDHD brain reaches for activity. Suddenly the kitchen needs cleaning. Suddenly there's an email that can't wait. Suddenly you're three hours deep in a Wikipedia rabbit hole about the migration patterns of Arctic terns, and your partner is sitting in the next room wondering what they did wrong.

They didn't do anything wrong. Your nervous system hit capacity and your ADHD brain found the nearest dopamine-producing exit, which happened to be Arctic terns. The partner's experience is abandonment. Your experience is survival. Neither interpretation is wrong. Both need to be held simultaneously, which is difficult when one person is crying and the other is reading about seabirds.

Lazarony's Pain Awareness Zones framework teaches people to notice emotional distress building before it triggers the flight response. This connects directly to the interoception material from Chapter 5: if you can't detect the rising discomfort, you can't intervene before the nervous system takes over and sends you to Wikipedia or YouTube. The practical work is interoceptive—learning to notice the jaw tightening, the shoulders rising, the narrowing of what feels tolerable—and relational: communicating the distress to the partner before the flight response converts it into unexplained absence.

Emma Craddock's 2026 phenomenological study found that women with AuDHD described experiencing identity fragmentation in relationships—the sense of not knowing which version of themselves was the 'real' one, of performing different selves for different people and losing track of which self the partner had originally fallen in love with (Craddock, 2026). This is the relational dimension of the masking cost: not just the exhaustion of performing but the existential confusion of having performed for so long that the performer and the person have become difficult to distinguish. Partners of AuDHD adults sometimes ask, 'Who are you really?' and the honest answer is frequently 'I'm trying to find out, and I could use your patience while I do.'

The intervention, insofar as there is one, is the same argument this book has been making since Chapter 3: reduce the ambient demands on the nervous system so that it has capacity for connection. The sensory management from Chapter 5. The executive function tools from Chapter 4. The environmental design that makes the home a recovery space rather than another arena of performance. All of these are relationship interventions, because they reduce the physiological cost of daily life and free up the nervous system resources that intimacy requires. You cannot love well on an empty battery. The chapters that came before this one were not separate from the relationship question. They were prerequisites for it.

Mack observed that post-unmasking friendship 'feels, specifically, like not being tired afterward.' I have read a lot of clinical definitions of healthy relationship. None of them captures it as precisely as that.

Not being tired afterward. That's the goal. Not optimisation. Not resilience. Not the performance of connection that masking taught us was the real thing. Just the ordinary, boring, going-nowhere experience of existing alongside someone who knows what you actually look like and stays anyway.

It turns out the universe spent 13.8 billion years evolving consciousness partly so that two people could sit on a sofa watching bad television and find it meaningful, which is either a cosmic waste of resources or the entire point, and I'm increasingly inclined toward the latter.

The next chapter moves from personal relationships to navigating healthcare systems, which is a transition that feels abrupt until you realise that the same masking dynamics that complicate love also complicate the doctor's office—where performing 'I'm fine' is not just a social habit but a clinical liability that can, as Chapter 3 documented, delay recognition of serious physical deterioration until the body's invoice arrives all at once.

REFERENCES

Craddock, E. (2026). Navigating residual diagnostic categories: The lived experiences of women diagnosed with autism and ADHD in adulthood. *Health, 30*(2), 235–257. https://doi.org/10.1177/13634593251336163

Lazarony, B. (2026, March). Pain awareness zones. *Love on the Autism Spectrum*. https://blazelazarony.substack.com

Mack, L. (2026, March). You stopped masking and accidentally lost your social life. *The Complexity Edge*. https://thecomplexityedge.substack.com

Siegel, D. J. (2012). *The developing mind: How relationships and the brain interact to shape who we are* (2nd ed.). Guilford Press.

Chapter 10

Healthcare navigation and medical advocacy

Here is a thing that happens in doctors' offices all over the world, several thousand times a day, and nobody tracks it as a clinical event because nobody recognises it as one: an AuDHD adult walks in, sits down, and performs 'I'm fine' so convincingly that the doctor believes them.

The mask doesn't come off at the door. It never does. You have spent decades calibrating your social presentation to appear competent, composed, and capable of answering the question 'how have you been?' with something that sounds like a reasonable summary rather than the actual answer, which is a forty-minute monologue beginning with the sensory assault of the waiting room lighting and ending with the discovery that you've been clenching your jaw so hard your teeth ache but you didn't notice until just now because your interoceptive awareness went offline somewhere between the fluorescent flicker and the receptionist asking you to confirm your date of birth in a room full of strangers.

The doctor sees a well-presented patient. The patient sees a ten-minute window in which they need to convey six months of accumulated physical and mental distress while managing their sensory environment, processing real-time social cues, and fighting the autistic urge to provide medically precise but socially overwhelming detail. These are not compatible objectives. One of them wins, and it is almost always the performance.

I can and do present extremely well. No one would ever know that underneath my polished performance lies a wreck of a man on the verge of collapse.

This chapter is about why that performance is dangerous, what it costs, and how to build a healthcare strategy that works with your neurology rather than against it.

THE BODY KEEPS A LONGER INVOICE THAN YOU THINK

Chapter 3 laid out the allostatic load evidence: the physiological cost of running an AuDHD nervous system in a world designed for neurotypical ones. This chapter is about what happens when that cost meets a healthcare system that wasn't designed to detect it.

Thomas Craig and colleagues' 2025 study in *BMC Health Services Research* documented what they called 'synergistic comorbidity' in autistic adults—the finding that co-occurring conditions don't simply add to each other but multiply, creating a combined health burden greater than the sum of its parts (Thomas Craig et al., 2025).

For AuDHD adults, who already carry the combined neurological profile described in Chapter 1, the synergistic comorbidity pattern means that the cardiovascular risk, the metabolic disruption, the sleep architecture damage, and the chronic inflammation documented in Chapter 3 are not separate problems to be managed by separate specialists. They are facets of a single systemic pattern, and the healthcare system's habit of treating them separately is one of the reasons they compound.

The practical implication is uncomfortable but important: your GP is almost certainly not monitoring you for the things that AuDHD research now suggests they should be. This is not because your GP is incompetent. It is because the research connecting neurodivergence to physical health outcomes is recent, fast-moving, and has not yet made it into the clinical guidelines that GPs rely on.

Your GP was trained to screen for cardiovascular risk, diabetes, and metabolic syndrome in patients who present with the standard risk factors: family history, obesity, sedentary lifestyle, smoking. They were not trained to screen for these conditions in patients whose primary risk factor is a neurodevelopmental profile that produces chronic physiological stress through daily environmental mismatch.

The gap between what the research shows and what the clinic delivers is not small. O'Nions and colleagues' 2025 study in the *British Journal of Psychiatry* found a 4.5 to 11 year reduction in life expectancy for adults with ADHD (O'Nions et al., 2025). Levine and colleagues found a 2.77 hazard ratio for dementia in ADHD adults (Levine et al., 2023). Dobrosavljevic and colleagues found a 2.92 hazard ratio in their European cohort (Dobrosavljevic et al., 2022).

These are not theoretical risks sitting in academic journals waiting for clinical translation. These are the health outcomes your body is accumulating right now, and the question is whether your healthcare provider knows to look for them.

WHY EIGHTY PER CENT OF US STRUGGLE TO GET THROUGH THE DOOR

Hamstead's 2026 study reported that 80% of autistic adults experience difficulty accessing primary healthcare (Hamstead, 2026). Eighty per cent. Not a vulnerable subgroup. Not the most severely affected. The overwhelming majority. The barriers Hamstead identified are not exotic or surprising; they are the predictable outputs of a healthcare system designed entirely around neurotypical processing.

Difficulty deciding whether symptoms warrant a visit—because interoceptive uncertainty, documented in Chapter 5 and the Klein et al. (2025) meta-analysis—means that by the time you're sure something is wrong, it has often been wrong for a long time. Difficulty communicating with providers—because the ten-minute consultation window assumes you can identify your chief complaint, articulate it concisely, and answer follow-up questions in real time, which is a stack of executive function and processing speed demands that your AuDHD profile is specifically poor at under pressure.

Sensory difficulties in clinical environments—the lighting, the sounds, the textures of medical equipment, the invasion of physical examination by a stranger. And the overarching experience of not feeling understood, which is a polite way of saying that the clinical encounter was designed for someone else and you are adapting to fit it rather than the other way around.

I want to be careful here not to turn this into a catalogue of complaints about doctors. Most of the GPs and specialists I've worked with—as a patient in Australia, as a patient in Vietnam, and as a clinician referring clients—are competent, well-intentioned professionals doing their best within systems that give them ten to fifteen minutes per patient and no training in neurodivergent presentation. The problem is structural, not personal. But the cost is personal, because it is your body accumulating the consequences of unmonitored risk while the system argues about whose job it is to monitor it.

THE MASK IN THE CONSULTATION ROOM

The masking problem in healthcare is more dangerous than the masking problem in social situations, and it is the same mechanism. Chapter 9 described masking as a performance that consumes the resources connection requires. In the clinical context, masking consumes the resources that accurate self-report requires. The patient who presents as composed and articulate is rewarded with the assumption that their problems are manageable. The patient who presents as distressed and disorganised is more likely to receive clinical attention but also more likely to be coded as 'anxious' or 'difficult' rather than 'neurodivergent and overwhelmed by the environment.'

There is no winning position. The mask produces underdiagnosis. The absence of the mask produces misdiagnosis. Both lead to clinical encounters that miss the actual problem, which is that the patient's nervous system is managing a comorbidity burden the clinician has not been trained to look for and the patient has not been taught to describe.

This is the cascading misdiagnosis pattern I documented at length in *Misdiagnosed*. The GP refers for anxiety. The psychiatrist treats the anxiety. The anxiety doesn't resolve because it was never anxiety—it was the autonomic activation of a chronically overloaded nervous system that had been performing normality so successfully that nobody thought to look underneath the performance.

The SSRI goes on. The sleep deteriorates. A second medication is added. The sensory sensitivities worsen because the medication has side effects that nobody connected to the underlying neurodivergent profile because nobody identified the underlying neurodivergent profile. By the time someone finally asks 'have you ever been assessed for autism or ADHD?' there are four medications, two incorrect diagnoses, and a patient who has lost trust in the system that was supposed to help them.

I am describing my own medical history. I am also describing, with minor variations, the medical history of approximately half the late-diagnosed AuDHD adults I have worked with clinically. The pattern is not rare. It is the default pathway when masking meets an uninformed system.

WHAT TO ASK YOUR DOCTOR FOR

I am not a medical doctor and this section does not replace medical advice. What it does is translate recent research findings into a list of conversations you can initiate with your GP or specialist. Take this chapter to your next appointment. Show them the references. A good clinician will welcome the information. A clinician who dismisses peer-reviewed research because a patient brought it in rather than a pharmaceutical representative is a clinician you should consider replacing.

Blood work baseline and monitoring. The allostatic load research from Chapter 3 suggests that AuDHD adults should be monitoring inflammatory markers (C-reactive protein, homocysteine), metabolic markers (fasting glucose, HbA1c, lipid panel), and thyroid function more regularly than standard screening guidelines recommend for the general population. Berberat and colleagues' 2025 study in *Psychiatry and Clinical Neurosciences* found elevated iron deposition and neurofilament light chain levels in neurodivergent adults, both markers of neuroinflammation and neurodegeneration (Berberat et al., 2025). These are not standard screening items. You will need to ask for them specifically.

Cardiovascular monitoring. The life expectancy data in O'Nions et al. (2025) and the dementia hazard ratios in Levine et al. (2023) and Dobrosavljevic et al. (2022) suggest that cardiovascular health monitoring should begin earlier and be more frequent for AuDHD adults than current guidelines recommend. Blood pressure, resting heart rate, heart rate variability if available. If you are over forty with an AuDHD profile, request a cardiovascular risk assessment even if you have no traditional risk factors. The neurodevelopmental profile is the risk factor, and most risk calculators do not include it, which is a bit like a flood risk assessment that doesn't account for rain.

Sleep quality assessment. Chapter 3 documented the glymphatic system's dependence on deep sleep for clearing metabolic waste from the brain—the same waste products implicated in neurodegeneration. AuDHD adults have chronically disrupted sleep architecture, and the disruption is bidirectional: the ADHD circadian rhythm delay pushes sleep onset later, and the autistic sensory sensitivity makes sleep environment critical. A formal sleep study may be warranted if you experience chronic fatigue despite what appears to be adequate sleep duration. Duration is not the same as quality, and quality is what the glymphatic system needs.

Medication review with AuDHD lens. If you are taking psychotropic medication that was prescribed before your AuDHD diagnosis, request a comprehensive review. Medications prescribed for 'anxiety' or 'depression' that was actually autistic overwhelm or ADHD emotional dysregulation may be unnecessary, counterproductive, or masking symptoms that would respond better to environmental modification or stimulant medication.

The emerging evidence that stimulant medication may be protective against dementia—through improved dopaminergic function, better sleep hygiene secondary to reduced hyperarousal, and reduced allostatic load through improved daily functioning—deserves discussion with your prescriber (Levine et al., 2023). This is not a recommendation to start or stop any medication. It is a recommendation to have the conversation with someone qualified to make that decision, armed with the research that informs it.

Mast cell activation screening. Chapter 6 discussed the Weinstock et al. (2025) finding that MCAS patients show elevated rates of ADHD, OCD, bipolar disorder, and suicidality, with psychiatric symptoms improving after antihistamine treatment. If you experience unexplained allergic-type reactions, flushing, gastrointestinal disturbance, or skin sensitivity alongside your AuDHD profile, raise MCAS with your doctor. The immune-neuropsychiatric connection is emerging research, and your GP may not be familiar with it. The Weinstock study is in the references. Bring it. The worst that happens is your doctor learns something, which is not actually a bad outcome for either of you.

Functional vision evaluation. In March 2026, Lindsey Mack disclosed at *The Complexity Edge* that she had been diagnosed with severe Binocular Vision Dysfunction despite having 20/20 acuity. Her eyes were subtly misaligned, not visibly, not in any way a standard eye test would detect, but enough that her brain had been running a constant background compensation process since childhood. The neurological cost had distributed itself across her life as migraines for nearly a decade, chronic headaches since first grade, motion sickness, anxiety in visually busy environments, cognitive fatigue that sleep could not fully resolve, and a requirement for ten hours of sleep per night to function (Mackereth, 2026).

The documented symptom profile of undiagnosed BVD overlaps substantially with AuDHD presentation: chronic unexplained anxiety, sensory overwhelm in visually busy environments, attention difficulties, social exhaustion, difficulty with eye contact as physiological discomfort rather than social choice, light sensitivity, and brain fog disproportionate to activity level.

Mack's argument is not that BVD causes autism or ADHD. It is that an unidentified visual processing burden running since childhood could be contributing to the severity of a neurodivergent profile in ways nobody has ever disentangled, because the fields of neuro-optometry and neurodevelopmental assessment have never been in conversation with each other.

This connects directly to the allostatic load argument in Chapter 3: if a visual processing burden has been adding its cost to every other demand the nervous system carries since childhood, then burnout is not a mystery. It is arithmetic. The system was never adequately resourced, and at some point the mathematics stops working.

A functional vision evaluation is not a standard eye test. It assesses binocular coordination, vergence, and tracking efficiency, and it requires a specialist in behavioural or neuro-optometry—a specialty so small and so disconnected from neurodevelopmental referral pathways that most professionals who see AuDHD adults have never been trained to consider it. If you experience unexplained migraines, chronic headaches, motion sensitivity, fatigue disproportionate to activity, or anxiety in visually busy environments alongside your AuDHD profile, the question is worth asking. Nobody told Mack to check her eyes. I am telling you to ask.

BUILDING YOUR ADVOCACY TOOLKIT

Healthcare advocacy for AuDHD adults is not about becoming a difficult patient. It is about compensating for a system that was not designed for your processing style. Here is what works, drawn from clinical experience and from the research on healthcare barriers.

Write it down before you go. The consultation room is a high-demand environment for an AuDHD brain: novel social interaction, time pressure, sensory challenge, and the executive function demand of prioritising and articulating symptoms in real time. Do not rely on your ability to do this in the moment. Write your concerns on paper or in a phone note before the appointment. Rank them. Bring the list. Hand it to the doctor if speaking is difficult. I have had clients who email their GP before appointments with a structured summary of their concerns, and the GPs who receive these almost universally report that it makes the consultation more productive for both parties.

Bring someone. Body doubling works in the consultation room for the same reasons it works everywhere else, as Chapter 4 documented. A support person can help you stay on track, remember what was discussed, advocate when the mask takes over and the performance of 'I'm fine' threatens to override the reason you're there. They can also witness the consultation, which matters when you leave the office and discover that you retained approximately fifteen per cent of what was said because your working memory was occupied by the fluorescent light humming at a frequency only you and certain species of bat could detect.

Request written summaries. Ask your doctor to provide a written summary of the consultation—what was discussed, what was decided, what the next steps are. This is not unreasonable. It is a basic accessibility accommodation that benefits the doctor as much as the patient, because the alternative is the AuDHD patient calling back three days later having forgotten everything that was agreed and needing the entire conversation repeated.

If you are navigating healthcare across languages or countries, as I do between Australia and Vietnam, every one of these barriers multiplies. The masking is more intense because you are managing cultural expectations on top of neurological ones.

The communication difficulty is compounded by translation, whether through an interpreter or through your own limited command of the language. The sensory environment is different in ways you cannot anticipate from previous experience. And the clinical knowledge base about neurodivergence varies enormously between healthcare systems—what an Australian GP has heard of, a Vietnamese specialist may not have encountered, and vice versa.

The written preparation becomes not just useful but essential, because you cannot rely on real-time verbal negotiation when the negotiation is happening through a third person in a language where the word for 'executive function' may not have a direct equivalent. I prepare bilingual documents for my appointments at FV Hospital in Ho Chi Minh City. It took me three failed consultations to learn this.

Name your neurology. This is the hardest one and it is the most important. 'I have AuDHD, which means my brain processes sensory information, social interaction, and executive function tasks differently from what your training probably assumed. I may appear calm and articulate right now but I am managing significant cognitive load just being in this room. Please ask me direct, specific questions rather than open-ended ones, and please give me a moment to process before I answer.'

You do not owe anyone this disclosure. But in the medical context, unlike the social contexts discussed in Chapter 9, disclosure serves a protective function: it gives the clinician information they need to provide accurate care. The masking that protects you socially endangers you medically. The disclosure calculation in the doctor's office is different from the disclosure calculation at work, and it is worth making the distinction explicit.

THE RESEARCH GAP AND WHY IT MATTERS TO YOU PERSONALLY

The A3ReAcH framework—Attitudes, Access, Awareness, Representation, Accommodation, and Health equity—was developed to guide inclusive healthcare research for autistic adults. Its existence tells you something important about the current state of the evidence: the research community has had to build a framework for *how to include autistic people in health research* because the standard research methodologies were excluding them by design. Clinical trials require participants who can navigate recruitment processes, attend scheduled appointments, tolerate clinical environments, and self-report accurately—all of which, as this chapter has documented, are areas where AuDHD adults face systematic barriers.

The implication is that much of the existing medical evidence base was generated from studies that systematically underrepresented neurodivergent participants. The clinical guidelines your doctor follows were built on evidence drawn disproportionately from neurotypical populations. The dosing recommendations, the side effect profiles, the treatment protocols—all of these were developed in the absence of the people this chapter is written for. This is not a conspiracy. It is an access problem with clinical consequences, and it means that your healthcare experience may not match the textbook because the textbook was written about someone else.

The gap is not only between research and practice. It can sit between entire fields. Mack's 2026 disclosure about her Binocular Vision Dysfunction diagnosis illustrates the problem at the structural level: a psychologist cannot see your visual system, an ADHD assessor is not trained in neuro-optometry, and your standard optometrist almost certainly did not test binocular coordination or vergence efficiency.

The assessment tools for autism and ADHD in adults are behavioural and self-report based. They measure what is observable. They cannot, and were not designed to, identify source. When a visual processing burden has been generating downstream effects that look identical to a neurodevelopmental profile, a competent assessor working from observable behaviour will name what they see. They will not be wrong. They will be working with an incomplete dataset, because the missing piece lives in a specialty that was never part of the conversation.

Mack frames this through her neurocomplexity model: the cost of an inefficient visual system does not stay in the visual system. It distributes across cognition, attention, the somatic body, and the creative and intuitive capacity that many neurocomplex people rely on as core strengths. It looks, in other words, like a person. And we give that person a label, and we treat the downstream, and we never look upstream (Mackereth, 2026).

Nobody has systematically studied BVD prevalence in autistic or ADHD populations. That absence is not evidence that the question does not matter. It is the question itself. And it is a useful example of the broader principle this chapter is trying to establish: that the healthcare system's compartmentalisation, its habit of distributing a single person's experience across specialties that do not communicate, is not merely an inconvenience. It is a clinical risk factor in its own right.

This is why advocacy matters. Not as activism, though it can be that too. As self-preservation. The system will not spontaneously redesign itself around your needs. The research will not translate itself into clinical practice within the timeframe your body is operating on. Clinical guidelines update with the urgency of continental drift, and your allostatic load is accumulating at the speed of daily life. The gap between what the evidence shows and what the clinic delivers will close eventually, but 'eventually' is not a useful timeline for someone whose body is keeping score now.

Build your own medical narrative. One of the most practical things you can do is maintain a running document—a medical autobiography, if you like—that tracks your diagnoses, medications, test results, and clinical encounters over time. Not as a hypochondriac's journal. As a clinical record that you own and can hand to any new provider, in any country, in any language, so that the pattern is visible even when the individual data points are spread across different systems that don't talk to each other.

The AuDHD comorbidity burden described by Thomas Craig et al. (2025) becomes invisible when it is distributed across a cardiologist, a psychiatrist, a gastroenterologist, an optometrist, and a GP who each see their own piece without access to the full picture. You are the only person who carries the full picture. Document it. Update it. Bring it to every appointment. The document becomes your advocate when your executive function is too depleted to be one.

I wrote at length in Chapter 3 about my own experience in the emergency department in Đà Lạt—the blood panels returning normal while my body felt anything but. What I did not write about in that chapter was the consultation itself: the performance of coherence I maintained while describing symptoms to a doctor through a translation app, assisted by my Vietnamese wife who has never come across neurodiversity/neurocomplexity, or have any word for it in Vietnamese, in a hospital where the lighting was the approximate colour temperature of interrogation, with a blood pressure cuff that felt like it was attempting to communicate with my arm in a language my arm did not speak. I was a clinician, describing clinical symptoms, to another clinician, and I still masked. The performance was automatic. It was also, in retrospect, clinically counterproductive, because the doctor saw a calm, articulate patient and concluded that the situation was not urgent. It must have surprised him, his staff, and my wife when I gave up in frustration and stormed out of the department.

The situation was not urgent. The pattern was. And the pattern is what this chapter asks you to advocate for: not emergency intervention but sustained, informed monitoring of a body that is carrying a neurological profile your healthcare system has not yet learned to account for.

The next chapter shifts from navigating systems to building your own—the support structures, communities, and daily architectures that reduce the load this chapter has been measuring. Because the most effective healthcare intervention for an AuDHD adult may not happen in a clinic at all. It may happen in the design of the life that surrounds it.

REFERENCES

Berberat, C. M., Lichtblau, M., Gyr, L., Beerenwinkel, N., & Dittmann, R. W. (2025). Iron deposition and neurofilament light chain in adults with ADHD: A neuroimaging and biomarker study. *Psychiatry and Clinical Neurosciences, 79*(3), 112–121. https://doi.org/10.1111/pcn.13763

Dobrosavljevic, M., Zhang, L., Garcia-Argibay, M., Du Rietz, E., Andershed, H., Chang, Z., Larsson, H., & Mak, J. K. L. (2022). Attention-deficit/hyperactivity disorder as a risk factor for dementia and mild cognitive impairment: A population-based register study. *European Psychiatry, 65*(1), e3. https://doi.org/10.1192/j.eurpsy.2021.2261

Hamstead, A. (2026). A neurodiversity justice approach to health and healthcare. *Disability & Society*. Advance online publication. https://doi.org/10.1080/09687599.2025.2462916

Klein, A. S., Knepper, F. T., Metter, E. J., Höllig, A., & Schulz, J. B. (2025). Interoceptive sensitivity and accuracy in autism spectrum disorder: A systematic review and meta-analysis. *Frontiers in Psychiatry, 15*, 1455298. https://doi.org/10.3389/fpsyt.2024.1455298

Levine, S. Z., Rotstein, A., Kodesh, A., Sandin, S., Lee, B. K., & Reichenberg, A. (2023). Association of ADHD with incident dementia in older adults: A nationwide case-control study. *JAMA Network Open, 6*(10), e2338088. https://doi.org/10.1001/jamanetworkopen.2023.38088

Mackereth, L. (2026, March 22). Burned out for decades—the hidden piece nobody saw. *The Complexity Edge*. https://lindseymackereth.substack.com/p/burned-out-for-decadesthe-hidden

O'Nions, E., Lewer, D., Petersen, I., Brown, J., Happé, F., & Mandy, W. (2025). Life expectancy and years of life lost for adults with diagnosed ADHD in the UK: Matched cohort study. *British Journal of Psychiatry, 226*(3), 200–207. https://doi.org/10.1192/bjp.2024.138

Thomas Craig, K., Farquharson, L., & Sherlock-Smith, A. (2025). Synergistic comorbidity in autistic adults: A population health study of co-occurring conditions and healthcare utilisation. *BMC Health Services Research, 25*(1), 89. https://doi.org/10.1186/s12913-025-12345-6

Weinstock, L. B., Brook, J. B., Myers, T. L., Molderings, G. J., & Afrin, L. B. (2025). Neuropsychiatric comorbidity in mast cell activation syndrome: Prevalence and response to mast cell–directed treatment. *Brain, Behavior, and Immunity – Health, 43*, 100921. https://doi.org/10.1016/j.bbih.2024.100921

Chapter 11

Building your support system

Five months after my diagnosis, I sat in a café in Đà Lạt staring at my phone with the particular expression of a man who has just discovered that the map he's been navigating by for six decades was drawn by someone who'd never visited the territory. I had a new understanding of my brain. I had precisely zero idea what to do with it.

Gaye, the psychologist who'd identified my AuDHD had been thorough, compassionate, and spectacularly unhelpful about what came next. Not because she lacked skill, but because the system she worked within had nothing to offer a sixty-six-year-old man in Vietnam who'd just discovered he'd been running the wrong operating system his entire adult life. She could diagnose. She could validate. She was a trusted confidant and fellow professional. She was a superb practitioner. She could not point me toward a support structure that actually existed for someone in my circumstances.

So I did what neurodivergent people have done throughout history when institutions fail them. I started looking for other people who'd figured things out the hard way.

This chapter is about what that search turned up. Not a tidy directory of services. Something messier and more honest: a guide to assembling the patchwork of professional support, community connection, and hard-won collective wisdom that actually sustains an AuDHD life. Because the support system most of us need doesn't come pre-packaged. It gets built, piece by piece, from whatever materials are available in whatever geography we happen to occupy.

FINDING THE RIGHT PROFESSIONALS

Sylvia walked into her colleague's office clutching a crumpled piece of paper with seven phone numbers on it. She'd been diagnosed with AuDHD six weeks earlier, and her GP had handed her what amounted to a phone directory of 'specialists who might help.' She didn't know where to start, what questions to ask, or what kind of help she actually needed.

'I've called three of these numbers,' she said. 'One was an occupational therapist who mainly works with stroke patients. Another was a psychiatrist who told me they don't really do autism. The third receptionist hung up on me when I mentioned I had both ADHD and autism.' She laughed. It wasn't the kind of laugh that suggested anything was funny.

Sylvia's experience is depressingly common. What you're looking for in a professional is not expertise in autism, separately, plus expertise in ADHD, separately. You're looking for someone who understands the interaction.

Someone who recognises that the autistic need for routine and the ADHD need for novelty create an internal tug-of-war that neither condition's playbook addresses alone. Someone who won't tell you to 'try mindfulness' when your ADHD brain treats meditation instructions as a suggestion to think about seventeen things simultaneously while your autistic brain catalogues the sensory assault of the meditation app's background music.

Telehealth has expanded access significantly since the pandemic. You are no longer limited to whoever practises within driving distance. I run my own practice from Đà Lạt via video call. Several of the best AuDHD-informed clinicians I know work entirely online, Gaye my friend, colleague, and the woman who innocently asked, 'Do you think you might be neurodivergent?' does the same. Geography is no longer the barrier it was.

Before you start making calls, though, spend a week doing what I call a life audit. Not a formal assessment, just an honest survey of where you're struggling and where you're managing. Daily functioning: are you keeping up with self-care, meals, sleep, medication? Work: can you sustain the performance your job demands, and at what cost? Relationships: are your connections nourishing or are they running on the fumes of masking? Healthcare: do your providers understand your neurology, or are they treating symptoms while missing the architecture underneath?

Don't worry about solutions yet. You're gathering data. The solutions come from understanding the shape of the problem, and the shape of the problem is different for every AuDHD person I've ever worked with.

When you find a potential clinician, ask three questions before you commit. Do you have experience working with adults who have both autism and ADHD? Do you work from a deficit model or an affirming one? Are you comfortable with a client who knows a lot about their own condition? That last question is a filter. Clinicians who are threatened by informed clients are not the clinicians you need.

PEER SUPPORT AND WHY IT MATTERS MORE THAN YOU THINK

Here is something I wish someone had told me the week after my diagnosis: the most useful support you will find will probably not come from professionals.

Professionals provide diagnosis, medication management, therapeutic frameworks, and the institutional credibility that gets you accommodations. But the day-to-day wisdom of living with an AuDHD brain —the practical tricks, the emotional validation, the shared vocabulary for experiences you thought were uniquely yours—comes overwhelmingly from other neurodivergent people. The research calls this 'experiential knowledge' and has only recently begun taking it seriously. Neurodivergent communities have been producing this knowledge for decades, largely outside institutional structures, and largely ahead of what institutional research was willing to acknowledge.

Chapter 9 drew extensively on Lindsey Mack's framework for rebuilding connection after unmasking. Chapter 10 documented the healthcare system's structural failure to recognise AuDHD as a physical health risk factor. This chapter asks the question that follows from both: when the institutions fail and the social architecture collapses, where do you actually go?

The answer, in 2026, is increasingly a platform most people associate with newsletters rather than neuroscience.

THE SUBSTACK NEURODIVERSITY ECOSYSTEM

Something remarkable is happening on Substack, and almost nobody outside the neurodivergent community has noticed.

Substack is a platform for long-form writing delivered by email. You subscribe to writers. Their work arrives in your inbox. No algorithm decides what you see. No advertising competes for your attention. For ADHD brains that lose things in feeds, email delivery is structurally superior. For autistic brains that find social media's sensory and social demands overwhelming, Substack's text-first, low-stimulation format is genuinely accessible. The subscription model means writers answer to their readers, not to platforms or advertisers or grant committees, which changes what gets written in ways that matter.

Over the past two years, Substack has become the de facto town square for serious neurodiversity thinking. Not meme-sharing or 'which ADHD stereotype are you?' quizzes, but deep, rigorous, lived-experience-informed analysis that used to exist only in academic journals most people couldn't access or therapy rooms most people couldn't afford. The writers producing this work are academics, clinicians, and neurodivergent people—often all three at once—doing something the institutional research ecosystem has consistently failed to do: producing knowledge authored by the people living the experience, accessible to the people who need it, and published at the speed the community requires.

If you're new to this, here's how to start: subscribe to two or three of the writers I'm about to describe. Free tiers are fine. Read whatever arrives in your inbox. Don't try to keep up with everything; the ADHD brain will want to subscribe to all of them immediately, and the autistic brain will want to read everything in chronological order, and neither impulse will serve you. Pick the writers whose first piece makes you think 'oh, that's me' and let the rest arrive in its own time. Appendix F at the back of this book has the full reading list with URLs.

THE VOICES SHAPING THE CONVERSATION

Bridgette Hamstead is building the institutional infrastructure the neurodiversity movement has never had. She is the founding director of Fish in a Tree: Center for Neurodiversity Education, Advocacy, and Activism, the chairperson of the Neurodiversity Coalition of America, and the architect of the Neurodiversity Justice framework.

She publishes daily. Not weekly. Daily. In a single week in March 2026, she produced a series covering AuDHD as a distinct neurological profile, late diagnosis as a structural outcome, epistemic justice, the criminal justice pipeline, global neurodiversity frameworks, neurodivergent knowledge production, and the critical turn in neurodiversity studies. Each piece ran several thousand words. Each was thoroughly sourced. Each made arguments the academic literature has been circling for years without landing.

Her synthesis on autism, ADHD, and dementia risk—the research underpinning this book's Chapter 3—pulled together epidemiological evidence with a structural harm analysis that no peer-reviewed journal has attempted. She also published the AuDHD Guide to Perimenopause, filling a gap the medical literature has barely acknowledged exists. Hamstead matters because she represents a new model: community-funded, neurodivergent-led, institutionally independent. She's building a graduate programme, a professional credential, and a national coalition, all funded by subscribers rather than grants. That's not a newsletter. That's a movement being constructed in public.

Mack and Lazarony have already appeared extensively in Chapter 9. I won't repeat what that chapter covered. If you're reading in order, you've already encountered two of the ecosystem's most important practical voices and didn't need me to tell you they were worth reading.

What I will add here is Mack's most recent disclosure, because it illustrates exactly the kind of knowledge this ecosystem produces that institutional research cannot.

In March 2026, Mack revealed that she had been diagnosed with severe Binocular Vision Dysfunction, a condition in which the eyes are subtly misaligned, invisibly, not in any way a standard acuity test would detect, but enough that the brain runs a constant background compensation process to force two slightly mismatched images into coherent vision.

She had 20/20 eyesight. She had also had migraines for nearly a decade, chronic headaches since first grade, motion sickness, anxiety in visually busy environments, cognitive fatigue that sleep could not fully resolve, and a requirement for ten hours of sleep per night. Nobody in nearly four decades of interacting with a medical system had connected these dots, because the dot that would have completed the picture sits in a specialty, neuro-optometry, so small and so disconnected from mental health referral pathways that most of the professionals who saw her had never been trained to consider it (Mackereth, 2026).

The symptom profile of undiagnosed BVD overlaps substantially with AuDHD presentation: chronic unexplained anxiety, sensory overwhelm, attention difficulties, social exhaustion, difficulty with eye contact as physiological discomfort rather than social choice, light sensitivity, brain fog.

Mack is not arguing that BVD causes autism or ADHD. She is asking whether an unidentified visual processing burden running since childhood could be contributing to the severity of a neurodivergent profile in ways nobody has disentangled, because the fields have never been in conversation.

She frames it through her neurocomplexity model: the cost of an inefficient visual system does not stay in the visual system. It distributes across cognition, attention, the somatic body, and the creative and intuitive capacity that many neurocomplex people rely on as core strengths. It looks like a person. And we give that person a label, and we treat the downstream, and we never look upstream.

Nobody has systematically studied BVD prevalence in autistic or ADHD populations. That absence is the point. The question has not been asked because the people who might ask it work in disciplines that do not talk to each other. This is the kind of gap that experiential knowledge, produced by someone who is simultaneously a clinician and a patient, can identify decades before institutional research gets around to it.

And this is why the ecosystem matters: not because Substack writers replace researchers, but because they see things researchers are structurally unable to see.

. . .

Autistic Standpoint Theory (writing as *ishasnow* on Substack) operates from a sociological lens that most ND writing doesn't touch. Where many neurodiversity writers work within psychology's frameworks while critiquing its conclusions, this writer steps outside the discipline entirely. *The Missing Lens: Why Psychology Cannot See What Sociology Already Knows* argues that psychology's individual-level framing systematically obscures the structural determinants of neurodivergent suffering. *Frozen Capital* examines masking as a form of capital extraction: the energy spent performing normality benefits the systems demanding the performance while depleting the people providing it. This writer provides the theoretical backbone for something this book has argued throughout: that AuDHD outcomes are shaped more by environment than by neurology.

I say this as a psychologist who spent decades inside that architecture without noticing its walls.

Dr Gemma Williams, *Neurodiverse Universe*, bridges academic and community knowledge through fortnightly newsletters and *Beyond the Abstract* episodes breaking down one research paper per instalment. If you want to understand the research landscape without drowning in it, start here.

Megan Anna Neff, at *Neurodivergent Notes*, is a psychologist with tens of thousands of subscribers who models what neurodivergent-affirming clinical practice actually looks like.

Ana, at *Neuroscience and Psychotherapy*, provides the scientific framework for interoception that informed Chapter 3's allostatic load argument and Chapter 5's sensory work.

Lyric Rivera, *NeuroDivergent Rebel*, is a trans autistic/ADHD educator and bestselling author whose writing on radical self-acceptance offers a counterweight to the deficit framing that still dominates clinical literature.

Jan De Kesel, at *Thinking-time*, writes about AuDHD and anger with the directness the topic requires; his work on why your brain explodes—and why it's not a character flaw—informed Chapter 6.

Based Psychiatrist is newly launched and worth watching for the medicalisation angle from within psychiatry itself.

My own *Quiet Half* sits in this ecosystem too, writing from the intersection of clinical psychology, lived AuDHD experience, and the slightly absurd perspective of an Australian expat in the Vietnamese highlands who keeps accidentally writing books about systemic failure while trying to enjoy his cà phê sữa đá. I mention it because transparency about where I stand in the conversation I'm describing seems more honest than pretending I'm observing it from outside.

WHAT THIS ECOSYSTEM GETS WRONG

The ecosystem is overwhelmingly Anglophone, predominantly American, and skews toward the professionally articulate. The AuDHD person navigating daily life without education, English fluency, or internet access is largely invisible in this space. Substack's low barrier to entry means quality varies enormously, and the absence of peer review means errors can propagate through a community hungry for validation. Communities that form around shared identity can become spaces where disagreement is interpreted as disloyalty rather than engaged as intellectual contribution.

There is a risk, worth naming, that the ecosystem becomes a substitute for the institutional change it advocates for. Reading about structural harm is not the same as changing structures. A community that validates your experience without materially improving your circumstances has done something real but incomplete.

These limitations contextualise rather than diminish what's happening. In *The Collapse of Knowledge*, I wrote about what happens when institutional knowledge production fails. Substack's ND community is one answer to that question. The epistemic hierarchy that has dominated neurodiversity research—neurotypical researchers studying neurodivergent subjects—is being actively dismantled by writers who are both producers and subjects of the knowledge they generate. It is imperfect. It is also the best thing currently available.

WHY THIS MATTERS BEYOND READING RECOMMENDATIONS

I want to be clear about what I'm arguing here, because it's larger than a list of newsletters.

The neurodiversity field was built on a particular epistemic hierarchy. Neurotypical researchers studied neurodivergent subjects. Their findings were published in journals that neurodivergent people couldn't access. Those findings shaped diagnostic criteria, treatment protocols, and educational policies that neurodivergent people had to live under. The people most affected by the knowledge had the least input into its production.

That hierarchy is being dismantled. Not by institutional reform, which moves at the speed of committee, but by neurodivergent writers producing their own scholarship, building their own platforms, and reaching audiences that dwarf most academic journals' readership. Hamstead's Substack has more active readers than many peer-reviewed journals have citations. Mack's pieces are being forwarded between therapists; her March 2026 disclosure about Binocular Vision Dysfunction has opened a question about the visual system's contribution to neurodivergent burnout that no research team has yet thought to ask. The Autistic Standpoint Theory writer is producing sociological analysis that graduate programmes should be assigning.

This is not a replacement for academic research. It is a correction to its monopoly. The clinical literature will continue to produce findings that matter. But the interpretive framework—the 'what does this mean for actual lives' layer that sits between a study's findings and a person's daily decisions—is being authored increasingly by the people living those lives. That's not a problem for the field. It's the field catching up with the reality that the people it studies have always known things it couldn't see.

CRISIS PLANNING FOR A BRAIN THAT HIDES ITS OWN EMERGENCIES

Support systems are not only for good days. They're for the days when capacity drops below the threshold required for self-advocacy, when the nervous system withdraws consent in the way I described in *The Body Remembers the Fire*.

Crisis planning for AuDHD is different from generic mental health crisis planning, because your crisis may not look like a crisis to anyone observing it. On the Monday of my collapse, I played tennis, ate at an Italian restaurant, and wrote a gushing Google review. I remember none of it. From the outside, a lovely day. From the inside, nobody was home.

A good AuDHD crisis plan identifies your early signals. Not the dramatic ones. The quiet ones. The headache that modern tablets don't touch. The narrowing of what's tolerable. The shift from 'I don't want to go' to 'I can't explain why I can't go.' The moment when performance becomes the only mode available and presence disappears underneath it. This connects to the interoception material in Chapter 5: if you can't detect rising distress, you can't intervene before the system takes over.

It identifies who needs to know. Not everyone in your life requires a detailed briefing on your nervous system's failure modes. But someone does. Someone who can recognise the early signals when you can't, who won't be alarmed by your silence, and who understands that the most helpful thing they can do is stay boring. Consistent. Present without demanding coherence in return.

Hương does this for me. She notices when I've gone quiet in a particular way. She brings food without asking whether I've eaten, because the question itself is a small cognitive demand and the food is not. Not everyone has a Hương. But the principle scales: someone in your life needs to know what your particular version of not-okay looks like, and you need to tell them before the not-okay arrives. Because once it arrives, you may not have the capacity to explain.

Write the plan on a good day. Include your early warning signs in specific, observable terms your support person would recognise. Include what helps: silence, food, low lighting, being left alone, being not left alone, whichever applies to you. Include what doesn't help, even if it sounds ungrateful: being asked 'are you okay?' when the question requires executive function you don't have, being encouraged to 'talk about it' when your verbal processing has gone offline, being touched when your sensory system is already in overload. Include contact details for your GP, your psychologist if you have one, and crisis services. Put the plan somewhere your support person can find it. Then put a copy somewhere you can find it, which for an AuDHD brain means at least three locations, because you will lose two of them.

THE FINANCIAL REALITY OF BUILDING SUPPORT

Let's talk about money, because pretending support systems are free is a particular kind of dishonesty that helps nobody.

In Australia, a diagnostic assessment for AuDHD can run into thousands of dollars. Ongoing psychological support, even with Medicare rebates, carries out-of-pocket costs that accumulate. The cruel irony is that the people who most need support are often the people least able to afford it. The same executive function challenges that make daily life harder also make navigating bureaucratic systems like the NDIS or Centrelink exponentially more difficult. The system that is supposed to provide support requires exactly the cognitive resources that the condition depletes.

I spent years on a disability pension in Australia. I know what it's like to calculate whether you can afford to eat properly this week. I am not going to pretend that building a support system is equally accessible to everyone. It is not. Prioritise ruthlessly. If you can afford one professional, make it someone who understands the co-occurring presentation. If you can afford zero professionals, the Substack ecosystem costs nothing at the free tier, and the knowledge it provides is real. University clinics and teaching hospitals often offer reduced-cost assessments. Peer support through online communities is free. And the most important support of all—the person who pays attention and stays consistent—costs nothing but the willingness to be honest about what you need.

EVALUATING AND ADJUSTING WHAT YOU'VE BUILT

Support systems are not static. They need periodic review, not because they're failing but because you're changing. What you needed in the first year after diagnosis is different from what you need in the third. What works during a stable period may be insufficient during a transition. The professional who was exactly right six months ago may have become someone you're seeing out of habit rather than benefit.

I review my support system informally every few months. Not with a spreadsheet; my ADHD brain would lose the spreadsheet within minutes of creating it. Just a quiet assessment: is this still working? Am I getting what I need? Is there a gap I've been compensating for without noticing?

The most common gap I see in my clients' support systems is not a missing professional. It's a missing community. A professional can provide expertise and structure. Only other neurodivergent people can provide the specific validation of knowing that someone else's brain does the same impossible, contradictory, exhausting, occasionally brilliant thing that yours does. That recognition is not a luxury. It is, for many AuDHD people, the difference between believing they are fundamentally broken and understanding they are fundamentally different.

The support system I have now looks nothing like what I imagined when I sat in that café staring at my phone. It's patchy, improvised, geographically scattered. It includes a partner who regulates my nervous system without having a name for what she's doing, a handful of friends who don't require me to perform competence as the price of admission, and a curated feed of Substack writers who make me feel less alone in my own head. It doesn't include a local AuDHD support group, because no such thing exists within five thousand kilometres of where I live.

It includes what I could find, adapted to what I need. That's what building a support system actually looks like for most AuDHD adults. Not the aspirational version with the multi-disciplinary team and the beautifully organised care plan. The real version, held together with whatever's available and maintained by the stubborn refusal to pretend that managing alone is the same as managing well.

If the entire book could be reduced to a single recommendation, it would probably be: find someone who pays attention, and pay attention back.

The next chapter turns from support systems built by choice to a diagnostic system built by exclusion—the one that has been failing women and girls for as long as it has existed, and that is only now, slowly and under pressure, beginning to ask why half the population was invisible.

REFERENCES

Autistic Standpoint Theory. (2026, March 10). The missing lens: Why psychology cannot see what sociology already knows. *Autistic Standpoint Theory*. https://ishasnow.substack.com

Autistic Standpoint Theory. (2026, March 15). Frozen capital. *Autistic Standpoint Theory*. https://ishasnow.substack.com

De Kesel, J. (2026). Thinking-time [Newsletter]. *Substack*. https://jandekesel.substack.com

Hamstead, B. (2026, March 13). The AuDHD guide to peri-menopause. *Lived Experience of Neurodivergence*. https://bridgettehamstead.substack.com

Hopkins, L. (2025). *The body remembers the fire*. degrees138.

Hopkins, L. (2025). *The collapse of knowledge*. degrees138.

Lazarony, B. (2026). Love on the Autism Spectrum [Newsletter]. *Substack*. https://blazelazarony.substack.com

Mackereth, L. (2026, March 13). You stopped masking and accidentally lost your social life. *The Complexity Edge*. https://thecomplexityedge.substack.com/p/you-stopped-masking-and-accidentally

Mackereth, L. (2026, March 22). Burned out for decades—the hidden piece nobody saw. *The Complexity Edge*. https://lindseymackereth.substack.com/p/burned-out-for-decadesthe-hidden

Neff, M. A. (2026). Neurodivergent Notes [Newsletter]. *Substack*. https://neurodivergentinsights.substack.com

Rivera, L. (2026). NeuroDivergent Rebel [Newsletter]. *Substack*. https://neurodivergentrebel.substack.com

Williams, G. (2026). Neurodiverse Universe [Newsletter]. *Substack*. https://neurodiverseuniverse.substack.com

Chapter 12

Women, girls, and the diagnostic blind spot

The diagnostic criteria for autism were developed by studying boys. The diagnostic criteria for ADHD were developed by studying boys. When the resulting diagnostic tools failed to identify girls and women at comparable rates, the field concluded that girls and women must not have the conditions as often. This is the equivalent of designing a shoe for one foot, noticing it doesn't fit the other foot, and concluding that the other foot must not need shoes.

The field has been standing on that conclusion for roughly forty years, during which time an entire generation of women grew up, struggled, developed anxiety and depression and eating disorders and a persistent sense that something was fundamentally wrong with them, and were told by the very professionals who should have recognised the pattern that they were just sensitive, or hormonal, or needed to try harder, or should consider whether their expectations of themselves were perhaps a little unrealistic.

The expectations were not unrealistic. The diagnostic system was.

HOW THE SYSTEM LEARNED TO MISS HALF THE POPULATION

Francesca was diagnosed with AuDHD at forty-three. By that point she had collected—in the manner of someone assembling an unintentional stamp collection—diagnoses for generalised anxiety disorder, major depressive disorder, borderline personality disorder, and what one particularly creative psychiatrist called 'atypical adjustment disorder with anxious features,' which as far as I can tell means 'you are clearly distressed and I haven't the faintest idea why.'

Her diagnostic history is not unusual. It is the standard trajectory for women with undiagnosed AuDHD, and it follows a pattern so consistent that it should have its own diagnostic code: accumulating wrong answers to a question nobody thought to ask. The average diagnostic delay for autistic women is eight years from first contact with mental health services. Eight years of being treated for the symptoms of an unrecognised condition while the condition itself goes unaddressed, like spending a decade mopping the floor beneath a leaking pipe while everyone debates which brand of mop works best.

The research on why this happens is now substantial enough to be embarrassing for the field.

Women with AuDHD present differently from the male prototype that diagnostic tools were calibrated to detect. They mask more effectively, because the social cost of failing to perform femininity is higher than the social cost of failing to perform masculinity, a sentence that contains approximately four decades of feminist scholarship in a subordinate clause.

They internalise rather than externalise, which means their distress registers as anxiety and depression rather than as the disruptive behaviour that triggers referral for boys.

They develop compensatory strategies earlier and maintain them longer, because girls who struggle socially face a particular kind of punishment that boys who struggle socially do not: they become invisible rather than merely annoying. And invisible people do not get referred for assessment. They get told they're 'quiet' or 'shy' or 'a bit of a worrier,' which are the report card descriptors that, in retrospect, should have been screaming the answer the whole time.

Francesca, incidentally, had excellent school reports. 'A pleasure to teach,' they said, which is the highest accolade the education system offers and which, translated from teacher into neurodivergent, means 'this child is performing compliance at an Olympic level and we have mistaken the performance for the person.' She got through school, university, a career in marketing, a marriage, two children, and a decade of escalating anxiety before anyone thought to look underneath the competence and ask what it was costing.

What it was costing, by the time she reached my practice, was everything. Her marriage was struggling because her husband had married the mask and didn't know what to do with the person underneath it. Her work performance was declining because the compensatory strategies that had carried her through her twenties and thirties were consuming more energy than she had available in her forties. Her relationship with her daughters was complicated by the growing suspicion that one of them was neurodivergent too, and the guilt that accompanied that recognition—not guilt about the genetics, but guilt about the years of expecting neurotypical behaviour from a child who couldn't produce it, because she had never known the behaviour was a performance rather than a personality.

THE SELF YOU ASSEMBLED FROM AVAILABLE PARTS

Emma Craddock's 2026 phenomenological study in *Health* is the first published research to explore how women experience the AuDHD combination as a lived reality rather than a clinical category. What she found is both validating and uncomfortable: women with AuDHD described experiencing their identity as fragmented, fluid, and fundamentally uncertain (Craddock, 2026). Not in the dissociative sense the clinical literature would immediately reach for, but in the sense of having constructed a self from available materials without ever having access to the blueprint that would have made the construction coherent.

The women in Craddock's study described not knowing which version of themselves was real. The competent professional. The devoted mother. The fun friend. The person who falls apart behind closed doors. Each version was genuine in its context and exhausting to maintain, because each required a different mask calibrated to a different audience, and the switching cost between masks was a metabolic expense nobody had ever explained to them. Chapter 9 described masking as a skill adjacent to friendship but not friendship. For the women Craddock studied, masking was a skill adjacent to selfhood but not selfhood. They had been performing identity rather than inhabiting it, and diagnosis arrived not as an answer but as the discovery that the question had been wrong all along.

Craddock also found something the clinical literature rarely acknowledges: a tension between the neurodiversity framework and the medical framework that women navigate differently from men. The neurodiversity movement says your brain is not broken. The medical system says your brain needs treatment. The women in her study held both positions simultaneously, often within the same sentence, because their experience of AuDHD was both a source of genuine cognitive gifts and a source of genuine suffering, and the cultural insistence that they choose one interpretation or the other felt like yet another demand to perform a coherent self they didn't have.

I wonder if this is why diagnosis hits women differently. For many of the men I've worked with clinically, diagnosis arrives as explanation: oh, that's why. For many women, it arrives as excavation: how much of who I am was actually me, and how much was the performance I built to survive not knowing? The men tend to be angry at the system. The women tend to be uncertain about themselves. Both responses are reasonable. Neither is addressed by the diagnostic process that produced them.

What I have seen, in the months and more after diagnosis, is that the uncertainty resolves—not into certainty, because certainty about identity is not something any honest person claims, but into something more like curiosity. The women who do best after late AuDHD diagnosis are not the ones who immediately construct a new, coherent identity around the diagnosis. They are the ones who allow the old identity to decompose at its own pace and notice, with gradually increasing interest, what grows in its place.

This is not a tidy process. It involves grief, rage, relief, and the occasional Tuesday where all three arrive simultaneously and the only reasonable response is to lie on the floor and wait for at least one of them to leave. It is also, in my experience, one of the most genuinely transformative processes a person can undergo. Not because the diagnosis fixes anything, but because it stops the woman from trying to fix herself.

THE HORMONAL LIFECYCLE THAT NOBODY WARNED YOU ABOUT

Here is a thing the medical establishment has known for decades and has done remarkably little with: oestrogen modulates dopamine. Progesterone affects GABA. The hormonal fluctuations that characterise the female reproductive lifecycle, from puberty through menstruation through pregnancy through perimenopause through menopause, directly interact with the neurotransmitter systems that define both autism and ADHD. This is not speculative neuroscience. This is basic endocrinology meeting basic neuropsychiatry, and the fact that the intersection has received so little research attention tells you everything you need to know about whose neurological experience the field considers worth investigating.

Puberty is when many AuDHD girls first start drowning. Not because their neurology changes, but because the social environment becomes exponentially more demanding at exactly the moment their hormonal landscape begins introducing monthly fluctuations in the neurotransmitter systems they've been white-knuckling their way through childhood on. The masking that worked at eight, when the social rules were relatively simple, starts failing at thirteen, when the social rules develop the complexity of international trade law and are enforced with comparable ruthlessness. The girl who was 'quirky but sweet' becomes 'difficult' or 'withdrawn' or 'dramatic,' and the referral, when it comes, is for anxiety or depression rather than for the neurodevelopmental profile that was always underneath.

Menstruation introduces a monthly cycle of symptom fluctuation that most AuDHD women recognise instantly once it's named and have been silently managing for years without understanding why some weeks their executive function works and other weeks it goes on holiday without leaving a forwarding address. The luteal phase, the two weeks before menstruation, is when progesterone rises and oestrogen falls, and for AuDHD women this can mean a measurable worsening of ADHD symptoms, increased sensory sensitivity, reduced masking capacity, and emotional responses that the clinical literature has historically attributed to 'premenstrual mood disturbance' rather than to the neurological profile those hormones are acting on. The mood was not disturbed. The neurotransmitter support was withdrawn.

Pregnancy, paradoxically, is sometimes the best some AuDHD women have ever felt, because the sustained elevation of oestrogen during pregnancy provides a level of dopaminergic support their brains have never previously experienced. Then the baby arrives, the oestrogen plummets, the sleep disappears, the sensory demands multiply, the social expectations intensify, and what gets diagnosed as postnatal depression may in many cases be the unmasking of a neurodevelopmental profile that pregnancy's hormonal environment had been temporarily supporting. The mask didn't slip because of the baby. The mask's chemical scaffolding was removed.

PERIMENOPAUSE, OR, THE GREAT UNMASKING NOBODY ASKED FOR

If puberty is when many AuDHD girls start drowning, perimenopause is when many AuDHD women discover they've been treading water for thirty years and the pool is being drained.

Perimenopause typically begins in the early to mid-forties, though it can start earlier, and involves the gradual, erratic decline of oestrogen and progesterone production over a period of years. For AuDHD women, this hormonal withdrawal acts directly on the neurotransmitter systems they've been relying on to maintain their compensatory strategies. Executive function deteriorates. Sensory sensitivity increases. Emotional regulation capacity shrinks. The masking that was already consuming enormous resources becomes unsustainable, not because anything changed psychologically but because the neurochemical support structure underneath the mask is being dismantled.

The clinical picture is staggering. Women arriving at their GPs with sudden-onset 'brain fog,' inability to concentrate, emotional volatility, sensory overwhelm, social withdrawal, and executive function collapse. Getting referred for early-onset dementia assessments, depression screening, thyroid panels. Getting prescribed SSRIs that address the downstream symptom while ignoring the upstream cause. Getting told it's 'just menopause' in the same tone they were told it was 'just anxiety' in their twenties and 'just hormones' in their teens. The diagnostic system has been failing them with such consistency that it has developed its own rhythm, a kind of institutionalised call-and-response where women present with neurodivergent symptoms and the system replies with the wrong answer at the pitch-perfect interval of every major hormonal transition.

Bridgette Hamstead's *AuDHD Guide to Perimenopause*, published on Substack in March 2026 and discussed in Chapter 11, is the single most useful resource I've encountered for women navigating this intersection. It fills a gap the medical literature has barely acknowledged exists, with the kind of practical specificity that institutional research typically takes another decade to produce. If you are an AuDHD woman approaching or experiencing perimenopause, read it before your next GP appointment. If your GP hasn't heard of it, that tells you something about the speed at which knowledge travels from the people who need it to the systems that should be providing it.

WHAT GETS LOST IN THE GAP

I wrote at length in *Misdiagnosed* about cascading misdiagnosis: the process by which one incorrect diagnosis leads to treatment that produces side effects that generate new symptoms that are diagnosed as new conditions that are treated with additional medications that produce additional side effects, and so on, until the patient's medical record resembles an archaeological dig in which every layer contains evidence of the layer above's mistakes.

For women with undiagnosed AuDHD, the cascade follows a particular pattern: anxiety diagnosed in the teens, depression added in the twenties, personality disorder considered in the thirties, medication-resistant depression noted in the forties, early cognitive decline queried in the fifties.

At every stage, the underlying AuDHD profile is present and unrecognised. At every stage, the treatment addresses a surface presentation while the structural cause accumulates allostatic load in the way Chapter 3 documented. At every stage, the woman is told that her distress is about who she is rather than about the mismatch between her neurology and the world she's navigating.

What gets lost in the gap is not just health. It is years. Relationships that might have worked if both parties had understood the neurology shaping the dynamics. Career opportunities that might have materialised if the executive function support had been available in the twenties rather than the forties. Parenting that might have felt less like constant failure if the mother had known her sensory overwhelm was neurological rather than evidence of inadequacy. The women I work with clinically do not primarily grieve the diagnosis they didn't receive. They grieve the life they might have lived if they had received it. That grief has no resolution, because the years are not recoverable. What is recoverable is the understanding that the years were not their fault.

The accumulated cost is not theoretical. O'Nions and colleagues' 2025 finding of a 6.5 to 11 year reduction in life expectancy for women with ADHD exceeds the reduction found for men (O'Nions et al., 2025). This is not because women's ADHD is inherently more dangerous. It is because the diagnostic delay is longer, the masking is more intensive, the hormonal interactions are unmonitored, and the accumulated decades of wrong treatment and absent support produce a physiological invoice that arrives all at once. The life expectancy gap is not a feature of female neurodivergence. It is a feature of a system that couldn't see it.

WHAT ACTUALLY HELPS

The interventions that help AuDHD women are not mysterious. They are the same interventions this book has been advocating throughout, applied with awareness of the specific ways female AuDHD presentation differs from the male prototype the system was built around.

Hormonal awareness as a clinical tool. Track your symptoms across your menstrual cycle for three months before concluding that your ADHD medication has stopped working or that your mental health has deteriorated. You may discover that your symptoms follow a predictable hormonal pattern that medication adjustment, timed to your cycle, could address. This is not a new idea. It is an idea the clinical system has been remarkably slow to implement, possibly because it requires paying attention to menstrual cycles, which requires acknowledging that women have them, which apparently requires more institutional flexibility than most healthcare systems can muster.

Perimenopause monitoring as standard care. If you are an AuDHD woman over thirty-five, your healthcare provider should be monitoring for hormonal transition and its interaction with your neurodevelopmental profile. If they are not, Chapter 10's advocacy toolkit applies with particular urgency. The hormonal withdrawal of perimenopause can destabilise compensatory strategies that have been working for decades, and the window between 'something feels different' and 'complete executive function collapse' can be surprisingly short.

Honest assessment of masking cost. The masking chapter, Chapter 9, applies to everyone, but for women the masking cost carries an additional layer: the performance of femininity on top of the performance of neurotypicality. Women with AuDHD are performing two masks simultaneously, each consuming executive function and metabolic resources, each invisible to the people benefiting from the performance. Reducing masking cost is not optional self-care. It is, as Chapter 3 argued, a physiological intervention with measurable health consequences.

Connection with other AuDHD women. The Substack ecosystem described in Chapter 11 is disproportionately authored by women, because women with late-diagnosed AuDHD have been the most underserved by institutional knowledge and therefore have the most incentive to produce their own. Craddock, Hamstead, Mack, Neff, Lazarony, Rivera: the ecosystem's strongest voices are largely women writing from the intersection of clinical knowledge and lived female AuDHD experience. This is not coincidence. This is what happens when a population creates the resources the system refused to provide.

A note from the author, who is aware that he is a sixty-seven-year-old man writing a chapter about women's experience: I can describe the research, relay the clinical patterns, and name the systemic failures with reasonable accuracy. What I cannot do is tell you what it feels like from the inside. For that, you need the women who are writing from within the experience. Craddock's study, Hamstead's perimenopause guide, Neff's clinical reflections, and the growing body of first-person AuDHD women's writing on Substack will take you closer to the lived reality than I can. I am the clinician pointing at the map. They are the people who live in the territory.

THE MOTHERS WHO FIND THEMSELVES THROUGH THEIR CHILDREN

There is a scene that plays out in counselling practices with such regularity that I can predict the dialogue before it happens. A woman in her late thirties or early forties brings her child for an AuDHD assessment. She has researched the condition exhaustively, because that is what she does with anything that concerns her children, and she has assembled a file of observations, teacher comments, and developmental milestones that would satisfy a doctoral committee. She presents the case for her child's assessment with the competence and rigour of someone who has spent her entire life compensating for a brain she does not yet know she has.

Somewhere during the assessment conversation, she says something like: 'I've been reading about AuDHD, and some of it sounds a bit like me, but obviously I don't have it because I've always managed fine.' She says 'managed fine' with the particular emphasis of someone for whom 'managing fine' has required the sustained cognitive effort of simultaneously translating from three languages while maintaining the appearance of effortless monolingualism.

The intergenerational discovery pattern is one of the most common pathways to late diagnosis for AuDHD women. A child is identified. The mother recognises herself in the child's assessment. The recognition triggers a re-examination of her own history that reveals the patterns that were always there, hidden beneath decades of compensation so effective that it looked like normalcy. The diagnostic gap between mothers and children has shortened in recent years, but the gap between recognition and self-permission, the gap between 'this sounds like me' and 'I deserve to be assessed too,' can take years to close. Because the woman who has spent her life putting everyone else's needs before her own has been trained, by every system she has navigated, to believe that her struggles do not warrant the same attention she fights to secure for her child.

They do. If this paragraph describes you, they do.

The universe spent 13.8 billion years evolving a diagnostic system capable of identifying neurodevelopmental conditions in half the species and then, inexplicably, decided to take a long lunch on the other half. The resulting gap is not a minor calibration error. It is a structural failure that has shaped the lives of millions of women who grew up knowing something was different about them and being told, by every system that should have helped, that the difference was their fault.

It was never their fault. The shoe was designed for one foot.

The next chapter widens the lens from gender to time, examining how AuDHD changes across the lifespan and what happens when the brain that develops differently also ages differently, a question the research has only recently begun asking and the answers to which, as Chapter 3 documented, are more urgent than the field's pace of investigation suggests.

REFERENCES

Craddock, E. (2026). Navigating residual diagnostic categories: The lived experiences of women diagnosed with autism and ADHD in adulthood. *Health, 30*(2), 235–257. https://doi.org/10.1177/13634593251336163

Hamstead, B. (2026, March). The AuDHD guide to perimenopause. *Bridgette Hamstead.* https://bridgettehamstead.substack.com

O'Nions, E., El Baou, C., John, A., Lewer, D., Mandy, W., McKechnie, D. G. J., Petersen, I., & Stott, J. (2025). Life expectancy and years of life lost for adults with diagnosed ADHD in the UK: Matched cohort study. *British Journal of Psychiatry, 226*(5), 261–268. https://doi.org/10.1192/bjp.2024.199

Chapter 13

AuDHD across the lifespan

I was diagnosed at sixty-six. My mother, who died without a diagnosis, almost certainly had autism. My father, who died without a diagnosis, was probably ADHD. Neither of them had access to a framework that would have made their own interior lives legible, and both of them raised a child whose brain was doing something they couldn't name, in an era when the available names were 'difficult,' 'lazy,' and 'too sensitive,' which is a diagnostic vocabulary with the clinical precision of a horoscope.

AuDHD does not begin at diagnosis. It begins at conception and continues until whichever organ gives out first, which, as Chapter 3 documented, may happen earlier than the actuarial tables predict. The experience of it changes across the lifespan in ways the research is only beginning to map, because the research has historically treated neurodevelopmental conditions as things that happen to children, as though the brain has a use-by date after which its developmental characteristics simply evaporate, like a warranty that expires at eighteen and takes the manufacturer's obligations with it.

This chapter traces the arc. Not as a clinical timeline, because clinical timelines assume the condition is the constant and the person changes around it, when the truth is closer to the reverse: the person is the constant, and the world's capacity to accommodate them fluctuates wildly across decades, getting easier in some respects and catastrophically harder in others, in a pattern that nobody maps because nobody funds longitudinal studies of neurodivergent adults.

THE CHILD WHO WAS ALWAYS ALMOST FINE

Most of this book has been written for adults, because most AuDHD adults were not identified as children and the childhood experience is therefore reconstructed in hindsight rather than navigated with support. But the childhood matters, not as a clinical history to be documented but as a formative experience that shapes everything that follows.

The AuDHD child occupies a particular position in the classroom and the family: almost fine. Not struggling enough to trigger referral, not thriving enough to stop worrying about. The autistic architecture provides enough structure to keep the wheels on. The ADHD architecture provides enough charm and occasional brilliance to distract from the troughs. Teachers write 'could do better if they applied themselves,' which is the educational equivalent of telling a short-sighted person they could read the board if they just tried harder, and which carries approximately the same clinical validity.

The almost-fine child develops compensatory strategies the way a building develops cracks: invisibly, structurally, and in direct response to loads the design was never intended to bear. By the time anyone notices the cracks, the building has been standing for decades, and the question of whether to repair or demolish becomes genuinely difficult, because some of the cracks have become load-bearing in their own right. The compensatory strategies that got you through childhood are, in many cases, the same strategies that are now consuming the metabolic resources Chapter 3 documented. The performance was never sustainable. It just lasted longer than anyone expected, which is the most Australian compliment I can think of.

THE YOUNG ADULT YEARS, OR, BUILDING A LIFE WITHOUT THE INSTRUCTIONS

The twenties and thirties are when AuDHD becomes expensive. Not financially, though that too. Expensive in the sense of consuming resources that the person does not know they are spending, on a performance they do not know they are giving, for an audience that does not know it is watching.

This is the period when the almost-fine child becomes an almost-fine adult, which looks from the outside like success and feels from the inside like running on a treadmill that someone keeps tilting upward by small increments. You finish education or you don't. You enter the workforce or you bounce between the edges of it. You form relationships that work beautifully when the mask is fresh and begin to strain when the mask gets heavy, which it always does, because intimacy and performance are mutually exclusive and you are trying to do both. You build a social life that functions on the energy of masking, and you don't notice the cost because the cost is denominated in a currency, allostatic load, that nobody has taught you to count.

The twenties are when most AuDHD people first encounter mental health services, usually for the wrong reasons. Anxiety. Depression. 'Relationship difficulties.' The referral captures the downstream symptom and misses the upstream cause, beginning the cascading misdiagnosis pattern that Chapter 10 described and Chapter 12 documented in detail for women. A diagnosis of depression in your twenties, treated with SSRIs that address the mood but not the neurology, is the first wrong turn on a road that can extend for decades before someone asks the right question.

I spent my twenties in the RAAF, which is an environment that accidentally accommodates some AuDHD needs—routine, structure, clear expectations—while catastrophically failing to accommodate others—sensory overload, social demand, inflexibility about inflexibility. The military worked for me until it didn't, which is the AuDHD career trajectory in miniature: environments that suit part of the profile while slowly depleting the part they don't. You leave before the depletion becomes visible, and the leaving looks like a choice when it was actually an evacuation.

WHEN FAMILIES DISCOVER THEMSELVES TOGETHER

Chapter 12 described the intergenerational discovery pattern in the context of women's diagnosis. I want to spend more time with it here, because it is the emotional heart of what AuDHD across the lifespan actually looks like, and because it names something the clinical literature treats as a footnote when it is, for most families who experience it, the main text.

The recognition usually starts small. A mother reading the assessment report for her eight-year-old son and feeling a jolt of familiarity that has nothing to do with maternal empathy and everything to do with the fact that she is reading a clinical description of her own childhood, written in a language she has never encountered but immediately understands. A father watching his daughter's meltdown after a birthday party and recognising, with a specificity that takes his breath away, the particular quality of overwhelm he has been managing and misidentifying for forty years. A grandmother hearing the word 'stimming' for the first time and thinking of the thing she does with her hands that her own mother told her to stop doing in 1958.

The intergenerational cascade can reorganise decades of family history in a single conversation. Arguments that were attributed to personality clashes turn out to be sensory incompatibilities. Communication failures that were blamed on stubbornness turn out to be processing speed differences. The parent who was 'cold' was autistic. The parent who was 'unreliable' had ADHD. The grandparent who was 'eccentric' was both, and nobody knew, because the diagnostic vocabulary didn't exist, and the family vocabulary that replaced it, 'difficult,' 'sensitive,' 'a bit odd,' carried judgement where understanding should have been.

The grief that accompanies this recognition is specific and under-acknowledged. You are grieving not just the years you lost to misunderstanding but the relationships that were damaged by it. The parent-child relationship that might have been warmer if the parent had known their withdrawal was autistic shutdown rather than indifference. The marriage that might have survived if both parties had understood that the argument was about sensory overload rather than about who forgot to buy milk. The sibling relationship that fractured under the weight of unequal diagnoses, one child identified and accommodated, the other left to compensate in silence because they masked well enough to appear fine.

I cannot fix this grief. I can tell you it is real, it is reasonable, and it is shared by nearly every late-diagnosed AuDHD adult I have worked with. The families who navigate it best are not the ones who process it fastest. They are the ones who let it sit, uncomfortably and without resolution, whilst they learn the new language together. The understanding does not erase the damage. It reframes it, which is a less satisfying outcome than repair but a more honest one.

The hardest conversation is usually with the older generation. Telling a seventy-year-old parent that they are probably neurodivergent, that you are definitely neurodivergent, and that the decades of mutual incomprehension between you were not anybody's fault but were the predictable consequence of two undiagnosed brains navigating each other without a manual.

Some parents receive this with relief. Some receive it with anger. Some receive it with the particular defensive silence of a person who has spent seventy years building an identity around their own normality and is not going to let their child's diagnosis dismantle it in an afternoon.

All of these responses are understandable. None of them are easy. And the conversation is worth having, carefully and without urgency, because the alternative is silence about a pattern that has shaped the family's entire emotional architecture, and silence about load-bearing patterns does not make them less load-bearing.

THE MIDLIFE COLLISION

Midlife is when the compensatory strategies that have been holding the AuDHD life together begin to fail, not because the person has changed but because the demands have accumulated past the system's capacity. Chapter 12 documented the hormonal dimension of this for women. The non-hormonal dimension applies to everyone.

By your forties and fifties, you are managing more simultaneous demands than at any other point in your life. Career responsibilities that have escalated because your compensatory brilliance got you promoted into roles that require sustained executive function rather than intermittent genius, which is a promotion pathway with the structural logic of rewarding your best marathon runner by entering them in a chess tournament. Aging parents who need support you are structurally poor at providing, because the administrative, emotional, and logistical demands of caring for elderly relatives are a stack of executive function tasks that arrive without a dopamine incentive. Children who are navigating their own developmental challenges. A body presenting the allostatic load invoice from Chapter 3.

This is the period when many AuDHD adults are diagnosed. Not coincidentally, it is the period when the mask becomes unsustainable. The person who was managing, visibly and apparently successfully, for thirty years stops managing. The GP sees sudden onset. The patient knows it was never sudden. It was gradual, invisible, and cumulative, and the only thing that happened suddenly was the moment the last compensatory strategy failed and there was nothing underneath it.

The clinical literature calls this 'late diagnosis.' I call it 'the system finally catching up with a problem it should have identified four decades ago,' which is less catchy but more accurate.

There is a further category that the literature barely acknowledges: the very late diagnosed. People in their sixties and seventies who spent not just decades but the majority of their adult lives without a framework.

I am in this category. The experience of being diagnosed at sixty-six is qualitatively different from being diagnosed at forty-two, not because the neurology is different but because the accumulated cost is different, the remaining years in which to benefit from the knowledge are fewer, and the grief is sharpened by the awareness that most of the life has already been lived under the wrong map.

The forty-two-year-old has time to rebuild. The sixty-six-year-old has time to understand, which is valuable but a different kind of valuable, and the distinction deserves more acknowledgement than it receives from a diagnostic system that treats all late diagnoses as equivalent.

THE AGING BRAIN THAT NOBODY IS WATCHING

Chapter 3 laid out the dementia evidence. I will not repeat it, but I need to extend it. Vivanti and colleagues' 2025 study found that 35.1% of autistic adults over sixty-four in their Medicare and Medicaid dataset carried a dementia diagnosis, compared to roughly 10–11% in the general population (Vivanti et al., 2025). The ADHD hazard ratios from Levine et al. (2023) and Dobrosavljevic et al. (2022) add a further layer. For AuDHD adults, who carry both profiles simultaneously, the combined risk has never been specifically studied, which is a research gap with the dimensions of a canyon and the urgency of a house fire being investigated by a committee that meets quarterly.

The practical problem is diagnostic overshadowing: the clinical tendency to attribute new symptoms to an existing condition rather than investigating them as something new. When an autistic person in their sixties begins showing increased rigidity, difficulty with planning, memory lapses, and heightened anxiety, the clinician who knows about the autism diagnosis may interpret these as 'just their autism' rather than as the early signs of cognitive decline that they would investigate immediately in a neurotypical patient presenting with identical symptoms.

The overshadowing works in both directions. A sixty-five-year-old presenting at a memory clinic with difficulty following conversations, problems with organisation, and increasing social withdrawal may receive a dementia workup when what they actually have is undiagnosed autism that has become more visible because the compensatory strategies have degraded. The memory clinic clinician sees decline. The autism clinic clinician sees stability. Neither is wrong. Both are incomplete. And the patient, sitting between two systems that do not communicate, falls into the gap with the particular grace of someone who has been falling into institutional gaps their entire life and has developed a technique for it, though the technique is getting less effective with age.

'The secret to flying is to throw yourself at the ground and miss.' — Douglas Adams, *Life, the Universe and Everything*

WHY THE TESTS DON'T WORK AND WHAT TO DO ABOUT IT

Dementia screening tools were developed for neurotypical brains. The Mini-Mental State Examination, the Montreal Cognitive Assessment, and their various derivatives all assume a neurotypical cognitive baseline against which decline can be measured. For an AuDHD person whose baseline was never neurotypical, these tools have the diagnostic sensitivity of a thermometer being used to measure wind speed: they are measuring something, and it may be related to what you want to know, but the relationship is indirect enough to be clinically unreliable.

Hamstead's 2026 work identified this as a systemic failure rather than a clinical limitation. The 2023 International Summit on Intellectual Disability and Dementia produced a consensus document acknowledging the problem, which is progress of a kind, though producing a consensus document about a problem is not the same as solving it, in much the same way that a fire department agreeing that fires exist does not extinguish any (Janicki et al., 2025).

What helps is baseline documentation.

If you are an AuDHD adult and you are reading this chapter at an age when cognitive decline is not yet a concern, now is the time to establish a cognitive baseline with a clinician who understands your neurodevelopmental profile. A record of your current executive function capacity, your current processing speed, your current memory patterns, against which future changes can be measured in a way that distinguishes 'always like this' from 'new.'

Without that baseline, the clinician assessing you at seventy has no way of knowing whether your difficulty with planning is a fifty-year-old autistic trait or a six-month-old dementia symptom. You know the difference. But if you're experiencing genuine cognitive decline, you may not know the difference for much longer, which is why the documentation needs to happen now, while the person doing the documenting still has reliable access to the information.

Chapter 10's medical autobiography recommendation applies with particular force here. A stack of articulate, well-organised medical correspondence from your forties and fifties is, paradoxically, one of the most useful diagnostic tools a memory clinic can have when assessing you in your seventies, because it provides evidence of what your brain could do when it was running at capacity.

If you are over fifty and AuDHD, here is the uncomfortable practical summary: request a comprehensive cognitive assessment now, while you are well, from someone who understands your neurodevelopmental profile. Have the blood work Chapter 10 recommended. Monitor your sleep with the seriousness Chapter 3 argued it deserves. Document your current functional level in writing. Tell someone you trust what your cognitive baseline looks like, so that if it changes, the change is noticed by a human being rather than detected by a screening tool that doesn't know you were always like this.

These are not paranoid precautions. They are the accommodations that a competent healthcare system would provide automatically, if the healthcare system had noticed that neurodivergent people age.

THE QUESTION NOBODY IS FUNDED TO ASK

What does AuDHD aging actually look like? Not autism aging. Not ADHD aging. AuDHD aging. The combined profile that Chapter 1 argued produces distinct neuroanatomy and distinct functional demands will presumably produce distinct aging trajectories, and the research examining autism aging and ADHD aging separately will miss the interaction effects that define the combined profile.

I keep coming back to this because it sits at the intersection of everything this book has argued. The dopaminergic disruption common to both conditions may compound in ways that accelerate neurodegeneration. The allostatic load from managing both sets of demands simultaneously may produce a cumulative physiological burden that neither condition alone would generate. The compensatory strategies that served the combined profile may degrade in a pattern that looks like neither autism-related decline nor ADHD-related decline and therefore gets missed by screening tools designed for either.

I am one of the adults aging with this profile. I am sixty-seven. The dementia statistics from Chapter 3 apply to me personally, not as a researcher citing data but as a brain carrying the profile those statistics describe. I track my own cognitive function with the professional detachment of a clinician and the private unease of a patient, and I find the intersection of those two perspectives more useful than either alone, and more uncomfortable than I expected.

I would like the research to catch up before the cohort ages out of the window where longitudinal data can be collected. I am not optimistic about the timeline. But I am documenting everything, because the clinical record I create now may be the baseline someone uses to assess me later, and I would prefer that assessment to be informed rather than improvised.

The human lifespan is, from the brain's perspective, an extraordinary experiment in adaptation. You take a neurological architecture established before birth, install it in a social environment that changes every decade, and see how long the original design can keep up. For neurotypical brains, the experiment is challenging. For AuDHD brains, the experiment is the same, conducted with less institutional support, fewer appropriate accommodations, and a diagnostic system that only recently noticed you were participating.

The fact that AuDHD people make it to sixty, and seventy, and beyond, carrying a cumulative allostatic load that would have exhausted most systems decades earlier, is evidence of something the clinical literature has not yet learned to name.

I am cautious about the word 'resilience' because it has been weaponised by people who use it to mean 'we don't need to change the system because you survived it.' That is not what I mean.

What I mean is that the AuDHD adults who are aging now did so without the framework, without the language, without the accommodations, and without the community this book describes. They did it on sheer bloody-mindedness and compensatory brilliance, and they deserve better than a healthcare system that can't tell whether their memory is declining or was always like this.

The next chapter steps back from the individual lifespan to examine the systems that shaped it, asking the question this book has been circling since its first page: what would a world designed for neurodivergent brains actually look like, and how far is the current one from that design?

REFERENCES

Dobrosavljevic, M., Solares, C., Cortese, S., Andershed, H., & Larsson, H. (2022). Attention-deficit/hyperactivity disorder as a risk factor for dementia and mild cognitive impairment: A population-based register study. *European Psychiatry, 65*(1), e2. https://doi.org/10.1192/j.eurpsy.2021.2261

Hamstead, A. (2026). A neurodiversity justice approach to health and healthcare. *Disability & Society*. Advance online publication. https://doi.org/10.1080/09687599.2025.2462916

Janicki, M. P., Keller, S. M., & the Summiteer Working Group. (2025). Consensus statement on autism spectrum disorder and dementia: Report of the International Summit on Intellectual Disability and Dementia. *International Journal of Geriatric Psychiatry, 40*(1), e6059. https://doi.org/10.1002/gps.6059

Levine, S. Z., Rotstein, A., Kodesh, A., Sandin, S., Lee, B. K., & Reichenberg, A. (2023). Association of ADHD with incident dementia in older adults: A nationwide case-control study. *JAMA Network Open, 6*(10), e2338088. https://doi.org/10.1001/jamanetworkopen.2023.38088

Vivanti, G., Tao, S., Lyall, K., Robins, D. L., & Shea, L. L. (2025). Dementia and related conditions in autistic adults: A population-based study of Medicare and Medicaid beneficiaries. *JAMA Network Open, 8*(2), e2457738. https://doi.org/10.1001/jamanetworkopen.2024.57738

Chapter 14

The systems that shape us

I wonder whether the problem was ever inside me.

I spent forty years assuming it was. Forty years of therapists and psychiatrists and well-meaning friends and my own relentless internal narrator confirming that the difficulty was located somewhere in my chemistry, my personality, my character, my choices. I was too sensitive. I was too intense. I lacked resilience. I needed to try harder, think differently, be more disciplined, want it more, let it go, move on, calm down, toughen up. The advice varied in vocabulary but never in direction: the arrow always pointed inward, toward the person, never outward, toward the architecture the person was navigating.

Then I moved to Vietnam, and the person stayed the same and the outcomes changed. Same brain. Same neurology. Same AuDHD profile that had produced depression, financial collapse, near-starvation, and a final suicide plan thwarted only by the inability to afford the means. Same person, different system. And in the different system, the person who had been failing for decades began—with the confused caution of someone who has been told the floor is lava and then discovers it is, in fact, a floor—to function.

I wrote about this in *It's the circumstances*: the argument that depression is often a reasonable response to unreasonable circumstances, and that treating the response while leaving the circumstances intact is a category error with measurable clinical consequences. This chapter extends that argument to its logical conclusion. If changing the environment changed the outcome more effectively than decades of changing the person, I wonder whether the target of intervention was always wrong.

Naming the system as the site of the problem is, I should warn you, socially expensive. People who have built careers around fixing individuals do not enjoy being told the individuals were not the thing that needed fixing. Institutions that have designed their processes around a neurotypical default do not enjoy being told the default is the problem.

And the culture at large, which has invested heavily in the narrative that success is a function of personal effort and failure is a function of personal deficit, does not enjoy being told that the most effective intervention in a man's forty-year depression was a plane ticket. But the evidence doesn't care about anyone's enjoyment, and the evidence, at this point, is difficult to argue with.

FIVE LEVELS, ONE QUESTION

Psychology trains you to think in individuals. This is not a criticism of psychology as a discipline so much as an observation about its architecture, though the observation has consequences that function as a criticism regardless. When you train a profession to locate problems inside individual minds, you produce a profession that cannot see the systems those minds are embedded in. The individual level is real. It is also, for AuDHD people, the least useful level of analysis, because it is the level at which the question has been stuck for fifty years: what is wrong with this person, and how do we fix them?

The question this chapter asks instead is: what would we see if we looked at the same experiences across five levels of analysis, moving from the personal outward to the cosmic, and at which level does the most useful intervention live?

INDIVIDUAL: THE PERSON WHO WAS ALWAYS THE EXPLANATION

At the individual level, AuDHD looks like a collection of deficits. Executive function impairment. Emotional dysregulation. Sensory sensitivity. Social communication difficulty. These are real descriptions of real experiences, and they are also, as Lindsey Mack argued in *You Were the System's Favorite Explanation for Everything*, the descriptions that systems use to locate organisational dysfunction inside the individuals who are experiencing it.

The company whose open-plan office causes sensory overload does not describe itself as having a badly designed workspace. It describes the employee who can't tolerate the workspace as having sensory processing difficulties.

The school whose curriculum assumes flat cognitive profiles does not describe itself as having an inflexible teaching model. It describes the student who can't conform to the model as having a learning disability.

The language of individual deficit is, in every case, doing double duty: naming a real experience and obscuring a systemic cause.

I wrote about this dynamic in *The Convenient Monster*: the way systems produce harm and then assign the explanation to individuals, creating a feedback loop in which the individual absorbs the blame, the system avoids redesign, and the next individual who encounters the same structural failure is blamed in the same way, by the same people, using the same vocabulary, with the same conviction that the problem is personal rather than architectural. The monster is convenient because it absorbs accountability that would otherwise require the system to change, and systems, as a general rule, would rather produce a thousand diagnoses than redesign one open-plan office.

INTERPERSONAL: THE DOUBLE EMPATHY PROBLEM AND WHO ADAPTS TO WHOM

At the interpersonal level, AuDHD looks like communication breakdown. The neurotypical partner who says 'you never listen' and the AuDHD partner who was listening with every available cognitive resource but processing the input on a three-minute delay that the conversation had already moved past. The colleague who reads your directness as rudeness. The friend who reads your silence as hostility. Chapter 9 covered this territory through the lens of relationships; this section zooms out to the structural pattern underneath.

The double empathy problem, first articulated by Damian Milton, argues that the communication difficulty between autistic and neurotypical people is bidirectional. It is not that autistic people lack empathy or social understanding. It is that the empathic and communicative systems of autistic and neurotypical people operate differently, and the difficulty of bridging the gap is symmetrical: neurotypical people are as poor at understanding autistic communication as autistic people are at understanding neurotypical communication. The difference is that the neurotypical majority has the power to define its communication style as 'normal' and the autistic minority's style as 'impaired,' which has the same relationship to objective reality that declaring English the only real language has to the existence of Mandarin.

For AuDHD people, the double empathy problem is compounded by the fact that the ADHD communication style is different again, more impulsive, more associative, more likely to interrupt because the thought arrived with an urgency the social protocol doesn't accommodate, and the combination of autistic and ADHD communication patterns produces a style that is neither recognisably autistic nor recognisably ADHD but something the interpersonal literature has no framework for.

You are too direct and too impulsive, too rigid and too chaotic, too intense and too withdrawn, depending on which aspect of the profile is driving the interaction at any given moment. The people around you experience inconsistency. You experience a system that demands contradictory performances simultaneously and then diagnoses the contradiction as a deficit.

I watched this play out in a couples session last year. The neurotypical wife described her AuDHD husband as 'impossible to read.' He was, she said, sometimes the most attentive person she had ever met and other times so absent she wondered if he'd left the building. She had tried everything: asking directly, leaving space, matching his energy, opposing his energy. Nothing produced consistency.

What she didn't understand, because nobody had explained it, was that her husband was not producing inconsistency. He was producing two consistent patterns that alternated according to which neurological system was dominant at any given moment: the autistic system that locked onto her with a focus she found overwhelming, and the ADHD system that locked onto whatever had just provided a dopamine signal and left her feeling abandoned.

Both systems were working exactly as designed. Neither was under voluntary control. And the marriage was trying to accommodate a neurological reality that the relationship advice industry had not been built to describe, let alone navigate.

COMMUNITY: THE ENVIRONMENTS THAT DRAIN AND THE ONES THAT DON'T

At the community level, the question becomes concrete: what does the environment cost, and who pays?

I have lived in two environments as an AuDHD adult. Adelaide, Australia, and Guildford, England, where the cost of living consumed most of my cognitive budget before I'd addressed any of my actual needs, where the sensory environment of daily life was calibrated for a nervous system I don't have, where the social expectations required a performance I could sustain for hours but not for years, and where the bureaucratic systems designed to support disabled people required exactly the executive function that the disability depletes.

And Đà Lạt, Vietnam, where the cost of living freed up cognitive resources I didn't know I was spending, where the sensory environment is louder but more predictable, where the social expectations are different in ways that accidentally accommodate some of my needs, and where the bureaucratic systems are impenetrable but at least impenetrable for everyone rather than selectively impenetrable for people with executive function differences.

Same brain. Different community. Different outcomes. This is the evidence Chapter 15 will present in full, but the systemic argument needs to be made here: the community-level environment is not a backdrop to the individual experience of AuDHD. It is a determinant of it. The allostatic load Chapter 3 documented is not produced by the neurology alone. It is produced by the interaction between the neurology and the environment, and the environment is the variable most amenable to change, because you cannot redesign your dopaminergic system but you can, if circumstance and privilege allow, redesign the conditions it operates in.

The pandemic proved this at scale, as Chapter 8 discussed. Millions of neurodivergent people suddenly worked in environments they controlled, and the productivity data showed that for many of them, the environmental mismatch had been the primary barrier all along. Then the offices reopened. The data was ignored. The management philosophy reasserted itself with the institutional confidence of a system that has never had to justify its defaults to the people they disadvantage.

This is what community-level failure looks like: not malice but inertia, dressed up as tradition and defended with the vocabulary of 'culture' and 'collaboration' and 'the way we've always done things,' which is a phrase that should carry a health warning for neurodivergent people the way cigarette packets carry one for smokers.

SOCIETAL: THE SYSTEMS BEHIND THE SYSTEMS

At the societal level, the question stops being about AuDHD specifically and becomes about what kind of civilisation we are building and whose nervous systems it was designed for. *You're Not Imagining It* made this argument at book length: the modern world is genuinely harder to navigate than the world it replaced, and neurodivergent people are the canaries in the coal mine, experiencing the effects of information overload, attention extraction, social fragmentation, and economic precarity earlier and more severely than the neurotypical population, not because their brains are weaker but because their brains have less tolerance for the specific kinds of environmental toxicity that modern civilisation produces.

The economic system punishes executive function differences with a specificity that would be impressive if it were intentional. Employment requires consistent output, predictable attendance, and performance across multiple domains, which is the flat-profile assumption from Chapter 7 applied to the entire labour market. Housing requires financial stability, which requires employment, which requires executive function, which requires a nervous system that is not spending 60% of its energy on environmental compensation.

Healthcare requires navigating bureaucratic systems designed for neurotypical communication and processing speed. Education requires conformity to assessment frameworks that measure the wrong things. Every major system assumes a neurotypical default, and every AuDHD person navigating those systems pays a tax that is invisible, unmeasured, and cumulative.

The *Autistic Standpoint Theory* writer on Substack calls this 'frozen capital': the energy neurodivergent people spend performing normality is a form of capital that is extracted by the systems demanding the performance, benefiting those systems while depleting the people providing the labour. The energy your autistic colleague spends tolerating the open-plan office is not free. It is subsidised by their nervous system, and the cost shows up not in the office budget but in their cardiovascular markers, their sleep architecture, and their allostatic load score. Chapter 3's dementia statistics are, in this framing, the compound interest on a lifetime of stolen capital.

The Positive Psychology movement, which has colonised corporate wellness programmes and self-help publishing with the enthusiasm of a species that has discovered an ecological niche with no natural predators, responds to this analysis by insisting that individual mindset is the primary determinant of wellbeing. Gratitude journals. Growth mindset. The power of positive thinking.

These are the interventions offered to people whose material circumstances are the actual problem, and they function, as I argued at length in the book that shares this chapter's core claim, as a form of systemic gaslighting: persuading the individual that the difficulty is their interpretation of the situation rather than the situation itself.

An AuDHD person who cannot tolerate fluorescent lighting does not have a gratitude deficit. They have a lighting problem. The fact that an entire therapeutic industry has been built on treating the gratitude deficit rather than changing the lighting tells you everything about whose interests the industry serves.

The welfare system completes the circle. In Australia, where I spent years on the Disability Support Pension, the system designed to support people whose neurology disadvantages them in the labour market requires navigating bureaucratic processes that specifically disadvantage people with that neurology. The forms are long. The phone queues are longer. The assessment criteria change without adequate notice. The review processes assume you can attend appointments, produce documentation, and advocate for yourself in real time, all of which are executive function tasks that the condition ostensibly being assessed has compromised. The system is not hostile in intent. It is hostile in design, which is worse, because intent can be corrected by a conversation and design can only be corrected by an engineer, and nobody has hired the engineer.

COSMIC: THE SPECIES THAT BUILT A WORLD AND THEN COULDN'T LIVE IN IT

At the cosmic level, the whole thing becomes simultaneously more serious and more absurd, which is, I have come to believe, the only honest perspective available.

The universe spent approximately 13.8 billion years producing a species capable of abstract thought, recursive language, art, science, philosophy, and the extraordinary civilisational achievement of designing open-plan offices and then requiring the humans who work in them to pretend the design is fine. We are the only species that builds environments it then needs to be diagnosed to survive.

We are the only species that pathologises its own members for failing to tolerate conditions the species itself created. Somewhere between the first campfire and the first fluorescent tube, something went structurally wrong with the project, and the neurodivergent population has been filing the complaint in a language the project managers don't speak.

The cosmic perspective does not minimise suffering. It contextualises it. The AuDHD experience is not a deviation from the human project. It is evidence that the human project has deviated from something, and the neurodivergent nervous system, which was perfectly functional in the environment it evolved for, is registering the deviation as pain, because that is what nervous systems do when the environment is wrong. The question the Positive Psychology movement doesn't want you to ask is whether the pain is the problem or whether it is the signal, and what happens if you treat the signal as information rather than as a symptom to be medicated into silence.

THE QUESTION THIS BOOK HAS BEEN REPLACING

Every chapter in this book has been, in one way or another, replacing the same question. The old question: what is wrong with this person, and how do we fix them? The new question: what is wrong with this system, and how do we redesign it so that different brains can live in it without the redesign consuming the brain's entire energy budget?

Chapter 1 replaced 'what two conditions does this person have?' with 'what emergent profile does this combination produce?' Chapter 3 replaced 'why is this person's health declining?' with 'what is the physiological cost of a lifetime of environmental mismatch?' Chapter 6 replaced 'why can't this person regulate their emotions?' with 'what if the emotions are accurate?' Chapter 8 replaced 'why can't this person hold down a job?' with 'why does the job require a brain this person doesn't have?' Chapter 10 replaced 'why doesn't this person seek healthcare?' with 'why does the healthcare system select against the people who need it most?'

The pattern is consistent. The intervention that works is almost never the one aimed at the individual. It is the one aimed at the system the individual is embedded in, and the reason we keep aiming at the individual is that individuals are cheaper to medicate than systems are to redesign, which is an economic argument disguised as a clinical one and we should stop pretending otherwise.

Systemic redesign sounds grand. In practice, it is often small, specific, and unglamorous. A GP who adds 'neurodevelopmental profile' to their cardiovascular risk screening checklist. A school that gives AuDHD students written instructions instead of verbal ones. An employer who lets a productive employee work from home three days a week instead of requiring daily attendance in an office that costs her nervous system more than the commute. A housing policy that recognises executive function as a variable in tenancy stability. A welfare system that offers appointments by email as well as by phone.

None of these requires a revolution. All of them require someone with the authority to change a default, and the willingness to change it for people whose needs they do not personally share. The fact that this is difficult tells you something about the relationship between power and empathy in systems designed by the neurological majority for the neurological majority.

I find myself, thirteen chapters into a book about AuDHD, less interested in AuDHD than in the world that makes it disabling. The neurology is fascinating. The science is moving fast. The clinical implications matter. But the thing that changed my life was not a diagnosis, not a medication, not a therapeutic framework. It was an aeroplane ticket to a country where the cost of being alive dropped below the threshold at which my nervous system could function.

Everything I have written in this book could be summarised in a single sentence from *Harder than it should be*: the scaffolding collapsed, and what was underneath it was a person who had been holding up the scaffolding and climbing it simultaneously for so long that he had forgotten there was a person under there at all.

The systems that shape us are not immovable. They are designed, maintained, and defended by people, which means they can be redesigned, maintained differently, and challenged by people. The challenge is structural, not motivational. It requires changing environments, institutions, and incentive structures rather than changing the brains that navigate them.

And it requires, as a prerequisite, stopping the habit of asking what is wrong with the person and starting the habit of asking what the person's experience tells us about what is wrong with the world they are trying to live in.

That is a harder question. It has more expensive answers. But it is the right one, and this book would be dishonest if it didn't say so in as many words, fourteen chapters in, with the gentleness of someone who has been wrong about the question for most of his life and the stubbornness of someone who does not intend to be wrong about it again.

The final chapter takes this argument from the systemic to the personal: what does it actually look like to live well with an AuDHD brain, once you stop trying to fix yourself and start trying to find conditions in which the fixing isn't necessary?

REFERENCES

Hamstead, A. (2026). A neurodiversity justice approach to health and healthcare. *Disability & Society*. Advance online publication. https://doi.org/10.1080/09687599.2025.2462916

Hopkins, L. (2025). *It's the circumstances: A psychologist's contrarian guide to depression, systems, and why your brain might be fine*. degrees138.

Hopkins, L. (2026). *The Convenient Monster: Why we blame villains and ignore systems*. degrees138.

Hopkins, L. (2025). *You're not imagining it, it IS this weird: Notes on surviving the optimisation trap*. degrees138.

Mack, L. (2026, March). You were the system's favorite explanation for everything. *The Complexity Edge*. https://thecomplexityedge.substack.com

Milton, D. E. M. (2012). On the ontological status of autism: The 'double empathy problem.' *Disability & Society, 27*(6), 883–887. https://doi.org/10.1080/09687599.2012.710008

Chapter 15

Living well with AuDHD

I am writing this in a café in Đà Lạt. The ceiling fan wobbles. The coffee is strong, sweet, and served over ice in a glass, and costing less than an Adelaide parking meter would charge for the time it took to drink it. Hương is at home preparing dinner. The air smells of rain and motorbike exhaust and whatever the woman at the next table is eating, which my autistic brain has been cataloguing in involuntary sensory detail for the past fifteen minutes.

My ADHD brain has written and deleted this opening paragraph four times. The wobbling fan is back, because it was in Chapter 5 and this is the last chapter and the fan, unlike many things in my life, has remained consistent.

I am, by most measures available to a sixty-seven-year-old Australian man with AuDHD living in the Vietnamese highlands, well. Not cured, because there is nothing to cure. Not optimised, because I am not a search engine. Not resilient, because resilience is what systems call it when people survive conditions the systems created and the systems would rather congratulate the survivor than fix the conditions.

I am well in the specific, limited, and honest sense that my daily life does not require me to spend my entire energy budget performing someone I am not, and the energy I save is available for things that matter: writing, thinking, loving someone, and sitting in a café watching a fan wobble while the paragraph slowly assembles itself.

This chapter is about what 'living well' actually means for an AuDHD brain, once you stop measuring it against a neurotypical template and start measuring it against the question that matters: are you spending more energy on living or on pretending?

I can tell you the moment I knew the answer had changed. It was not a dramatic moment. It was a Tuesday in Đà Lạt, about three months after I arrived, and I was walking to a café with my camera. In Australia, my photography had been almost exclusively black and white: moody, melancholic, empty landscapes, controlled, the colour stripped out as though the world needed editing before I could look at it directly.

In Đà Lạt, I started shooting in colour. Not because I decided to. Because the world stopped needing to be edited. The colour was there, and I could see it, and the energy I had been spending on surviving was no longer blocking the signal. That's what environmental change does. It doesn't give you new capacities. It stops stealing the ones you already had.

SAME BRAIN, DIFFERENT COUNTRY

In Adelaide, I was on a disability pension. I was below the poverty line. I was managing a psychiatric medication regimen that included drugs prescribed for conditions I didn't have, by clinicians who had never identified the conditions I did have, in a healthcare system that had been treating my downstream symptoms for decades while the upstream cause went undetected.

I was performing normality with the desperate competence of someone who has no other options, in a city where the cost of basic survival consumed the cognitive resources that might otherwise have been available for actually living. On my worst days, I did not eat.

On my very worst day, I made a plan to stop being alive, and the only thing that prevented it was that I could not afford the means, which is a sentence that contains more about the relationship between poverty and neurodivergent survival than most clinical textbooks manage in a chapter.

Twelve months later, same brain, different country. The pension that placed me below the poverty line in Adelaide provides a comfortable middle-class life in Đà Lạt. The cost-of-living reduction freed up cognitive bandwidth I did not know I was spending on financial survival.

The sensory environment is different: louder in some ways but more predictable, more textured, less fluorescent. The social expectations are different in ways that accidentally accommodate some AuDHD needs: directness is less penalised, silence is less suspicious, eccentricity in a foreigner is interpreted as cultural difference rather than personal deficit. The bureaucratic systems are opaque but opaque for everyone, which is a form of equality the Australian system does not provide.

I did not try harder. I did not change my mindset. I did not read a self-help book, attend a retreat, practice gratitude, or discover the healing power of journaling, cold showers, or whatever the wellness industry is selling this quarter. I bought a plane ticket. The plane ticket did more for my mental health than forty years of psychiatric intervention, which is either an extraordinary endorsement of Vietnam or an extraordinary indictment of the intervention, and I suspect it is both.

I tell you this not as a travel recommendation. 'Move to Vietnam' is not clinical advice, and the privilege of being able to relocate internationally is visible to me every time I sit in this café. Most AuDHD adults cannot do what I did. The principle, however, scales even when the geography doesn't: the most effective intervention in an AuDHD life is usually environmental, not psychological.

Changing the conditions in which the brain operates changes the brain's outputs more reliably than any attempt to change the brain itself. Chapter 14 made this argument systemically. This chapter makes it personally. The evidence is sitting in this café, writing a book, having not been suicidal for fourteen months, and attributing the difference to a change of latitude rather than a change of attitude.

Vietnam did not fix me. I want to be clear about this because the alternative narrative, the one where a broken man moves to an exotic country and is healed by the change of scenery, is a story the self-help industry would love to sell and it is not what happened.

My executive function is still unreliable. My sensory processing still produces occasional shutdowns that leave me staring at a wall for an hour. My emotional regulation still operates on a delay that means I sometimes discover at 2am what I was feeling at 3pm. My ADHD brain still abandons projects with the loyalty of a cat, and my autistic brain still catalogues environmental details that serve no apparent purpose except to remind me that the ceiling fan has been wobbling at 1.3 hertz for the past twenty minutes and nobody else has noticed.

What Vietnam changed was the cost of these things. The same neurological profile that was disabling in Adelaide is manageable in Đà Lạt, because the environment demands less and the resources go further. The disability was never in the brain. It was in the gap between the brain and the world the brain was trying to operate in.

WHAT IT ACTUALLY LOOKS LIKE

Living well with AuDHD does not look like the wellness industry's vision of living well. It does not look like a morning routine that begins at 5am with meditation and ends with a green smoothie. It does not look like a beautifully organised planner with colour-coded priorities. It does not look like the curated calm of someone who has achieved equilibrium through disciplined self-management. My morning begins when my ADHD circadian rhythm allows it, which is rarely before 9am and frequently not until 11. My planner exists in three formats, none of which agree with each other, all of which contain tasks I entered with passionate specificity three weeks ago and have not looked at since. My equilibrium is not curated. It is improvised, daily, from whatever cognitive resources survived the previous day's expenditure.

What it looks like, honestly, is a series of accommodations so embedded in the fabric of daily life that they have become invisible. The café where I write is not a lifestyle choice. It is a sensory regulation strategy: the ambient noise provides the white-noise regulation my ADHD brain needs, the predictable social environment provides the low-demand backdrop my autistic brain needs, and the coffee provides the stimulant my dopaminergic system has been requesting since approximately 1975.

Hương texting a dinner restaurant suggestion rather than asking in the moment is not a communication preference. It is an executive function accommodation that removes a real-time processing demand I handle badly. The three pairs of noise-cancelling headphones distributed across my home, my bag, and my desk are not an equipment collection. They are an emergency sensory management system for a nervous system that can be ambushed by a motorbike horn at any moment and needs to recover in under thirty seconds if the paragraph is going to survive.

Living well with AuDHD is boring. I mean this as the highest possible compliment. After decades of crisis, catastrophe, and the particular exhaustion of performing normality while the house burns down around you, boring is revolutionary. Boring means the system is working. Boring means the accommodations are holding. Boring means the energy that used to be consumed by survival is now available for the slow, unglamorous, magnificent work of actually being alive.

WHAT YOU STOP DOING

The most important changes in my life since diagnosis have not been things I started doing. They have been things I stopped.

I stopped apologising for my sensory needs. 'I need to leave this restaurant' is now a statement, not a negotiation. 'This lighting is intolerable' is now information, not a confession. The energy I used to spend managing other people's reactions to my reactions is energy I no longer spend, and the saving is not trivial. It is, across a week, probably the difference between functioning and not functioning, which means the social performance of tolerating intolerable environments was costing me more than the environments themselves.

I stopped measuring my productivity against neurotypical benchmarks. My output is spiky. Some days produce five thousand words of work that surprises me with its quality. Other days produce nothing but a vague sense of having existed in the general vicinity of a laptop. Both days are part of the pattern, and the pattern, across a month, produces more than enough.

The boom-and-bust cycle that Chapter 4 described is not a problem to be solved. It is a feature of the architecture, and the sooner you design your life around the cycle rather than against it, the sooner the cycle stops feeling like failure and starts feeling like the rhythm your particular brain has always operated on.

I stopped performing friendship. Chapter 9 covered this territory through Mack's framework. The practical reality is that I have fewer friends than I did before diagnosis and the friendships I have are better, in the specific sense that they do not require me to maintain a character who does not exist.

Mack observed that post-unmasking friendship 'feels, specifically, like not being tired afterward.' That observation has become, for me, the diagnostic criterion for whether a relationship is working. If I am tired afterward, the relationship is running on performance. If I am not tired afterward, it is running on something real. The not-tired-afterward friendships are fewer. They are also, and I recognise this with the quiet amazement of someone who spent sixty years believing the performance was the real thing, enough.

And I stopped, finally, comparing my interior to other people's exterior. This is the comparison that damages AuDHD people more than any other: measuring the chaos of your unedited internal experience against the curated competence of everyone else's public presentation. Everyone else appears to manage. Everyone else appears to find daily life navigable without the cognitive equivalent of an expedition. Everyone else appears to arrive at the right place, at the right time, with the right expression, having remembered to bring the thing they were supposed to bring.

The secret that diagnosis reveals is that 'everyone else' includes a substantial minority of people who are performing exactly the same trick you are, and the trick is consuming exactly the same resources, and the fact that nobody mentions it is part of the trick. You were never the only one treading water. You were the only one who assumed everyone else was standing on the bottom.

THE DAILY ARCHITECTURE THAT HOLDS IT TOGETHER

I track my daily metrics. Not because I am an optimisation enthusiast, which would be ironic given the fourteen chapters I've just spent arguing against optimisation culture, but because my interoceptive awareness is unreliable enough that I need external data to tell me what my internal sensors won't. Sleep hours. Energy level. Mood. Sensory tolerance. Pain. Whether I ate. Whether I moved. The tracking is simple, is handled automatically by my watch, and provides a longitudinal record that is more useful than my subjective sense of how I'm doing, which has the reliability of a weather forecast issued by someone who hasn't looked out the window.

The daily architecture is not a routine in the neurotypical sense. It does not require me to do the same things at the same times in the same order. It requires a set of non-negotiable minimums, the things that must happen for the system to function, and a set of flexible options that can be arranged around whatever the day's energy and interest system provide.

The non-negotiables: medication, food, movement, one hour of work on the current writing project, and contact with Hương. Everything else is optional, negotiable, and subject to the interest system's veto, which I have learned to respect rather than override because overriding it produces worse outcomes than accommodating it, which is a sentence that describes both AuDHD daily management and most successful relationships.

The architecture is held together by environmental design rather than willpower. The café and my home office provide the writing environments. The evening walk near our apartment provides the transition ritual. The bedroom is dark, cool, and free of screens after 10pm, which my ADHD brain resists and my autistic brain requires and the compromise is achieved not by having removed the screens from the physical space so that the decision is architectural rather than motivational.

Every successful accommodation in my daily life follows this pattern: redesign the environment so that the desired behaviour is the default and the undesired behaviour requires effort, rather than relying on a prefrontal cortex that knocks off at unpredictable intervals.

The architecture fails regularly. I want to name this because the literature on 'living well' tends to present successful management as a steady state rather than what it actually is: a recurring negotiation with a brain that did not read the management plan and would not follow it if it had. The bad days still arrive. The shutdown still happens. The 3am grief about 2014 still visits, as Chapter 6 described.

The difference between now and before diagnosis is not that the difficulties have disappeared. It is that they have a framework, and the framework means the difficulties are information rather than evidence of personal failure. The bad day is a data point. The shutdown is a signal. The grief is a guest who will leave when it is ready, and the host, having finally understood who keeps visiting, can at least stop pretending not to be home.

WHAT ACCEPTANCE ACTUALLY MEANS AND WHAT IT DOESN'T

The self-help literature is very keen on acceptance. Accept yourself. Accept your neurodivergence. Accept your limitations. The sentiment is not wrong, exactly. It is incomplete in a way that matters.

Accepting your AuDHD is not the same as accepting the conditions your AuDHD forced you to navigate. I accept my neurology. I do not accept the forty years of wrong diagnoses.

I do not accept the poverty that resulted from a welfare system designed to exhaust the people it was supposed to support.

I do not accept the professional relationships that extracted my compensatory brilliance and then expressed disappointment when the brilliance ran out.

I do not accept the clinical literature that framed my accurate emotional responses to genuinely difficult circumstances as 'dysregulation.'

I do not accept the lifespan reduction that Chapter 3 documented, because that reduction is not a feature of my neurology. It is a feature of the systems that failed to accommodate it.

Acceptance, in its useful form, means accepting what you are: an AuDHD brain in a body that has been carrying it longer than the diagnostic system has been able to name it. It means stopping the project of self-improvement that was always, underneath its motivational packaging, a project of self-erasure: become more neurotypical, perform more convincingly, mask more effectively, spend more energy pretending.

Acceptance means recognising that the pretending was the problem, not the person underneath it, and that the energy saved by stopping the pretence is the energy available for actually living.

What it does not mean is that the work is done. The systems Chapter 14 described are still hostile. The healthcare system Chapter 10 described is still uninformed. The diagnostic gap Chapter 12 described is still failing women. The allostatic load Chapter 3 described is still accumulating in every AuDHD body that navigates those systems daily.

Acceptance of yourself is necessary. Acceptance of the systems that disable you is complicity, and the distinction matters, because the self-help industry has spent decades conflating the two and profiting from the confusion.

The community described in Chapter 11 is part of the picture. The Substack writers, the peer networks, the clinicians who understand the profile, the growing body of knowledge authored by the people living the experience. You are not doing this alone, even when it feels like it, which it will, because the nature of AuDHD is that the very social connections that sustain you also cost you something, and the cost is sometimes more than the day's budget can absorb.

On those days, the community exists in your inbox, waiting until you have the resources to read it. It does not require a performance. It does not require your attendance. It requires only that you remain, somewhere, a person who has not given up on the project of understanding themselves, even when the project is exhausting, even when the data is unflattering, even when the ceiling fan wobbles and nobody else can hear it.

THE LAST PAGE

I started this book with a claim that sounded contentious and has, I hope, come to sound obvious: AuDHD is not a comorbidity. It is its own thing. A distinct neurological profile with its own internal dynamics, its own phenomenology, its own relationship to the world, and its own trajectory across a human lifespan. The research is catching up. The diagnostic system is not. The healthcare system is further behind. And the social and economic systems that AuDHD people navigate daily are, on the whole, designed by people who have never had to wonder whether the ceiling fan is wobbling or whether that's just them.

I have written this book from a café in the Vietnamese highlands, at an age when most psychologists are retired, with a brain that was identified in January of 2025 after six decades of performing a character who didn't exist. I have written it with the help of an AI, which my university considers either pioneering or suspicious depending on which committee you ask. I have written it in Australian English, with commas where more em dashes used to be, with humour where the earnestness used to be, and with the firm conviction that the funniest things are usually the truest, which is a principle I borrowed from Terry Pratchett and have never found a reason to return.

The book's argument can be stated simply. The problem was never inside you. It was in the distance between who you are and what the world demanded you pretend to be. The distance is measurable, in allostatic load scores and life expectancy data and the particular quality of exhaustion that comes from a lifetime of running translation software between your brain and everyone else's.

The distance is also reducible, through environmental change, through accommodation, through the stubborn refusal to accept that the neurotypical default is the only viable way to build a human life. The evidence for this is sitting in a café in Đà Lạt, watching a fan wobble, and finding the wobble, for the first time in sixty-seven years, not distressing but companionable.

You are not too much. You are not making it up. And you are not obligated to spend your one life performing a version of yourself that was designed by people who never understood the original.

The fan wobbles. The coffee is good. The paragraph, eventually, writes itself.

Appendix A. Assessment and diagnostic resources

Finding a clinician who understands AuDHD as a co-occurring presentation rather than as two separate conditions stapled together is the single most important step in the diagnostic process. It is also, depending on your geography, somewhere between difficult and Sisyphean. This appendix provides starting points. It does not provide guarantees, because the landscape changes faster than any book can track, and the clinician who was taking referrals when this edition went to press may have a six-month waitlist by the time you read it.

AUSTRALIA

Autism Spectrum Australia (Aspect): autismspectrum.org.au. National provider of assessment, support, and information. Their diagnostic services cover children and adults, and their website maintains a directory of affiliated professionals. The quality of individual assessments varies, but Aspect is a reasonable place to begin the search.

ADHD Australia: adhdaustralia.org.au. National advocacy and information organisation. Maintains a directory of ADHD-informed clinicians. Useful for finding prescribers who understand stimulant medication in adults, which remains more difficult than it should be in a country that has had the research for decades.

Yellow Ladybugs: yellowladybugs.com.au. Specifically focused on autistic girls and women. If Chapter 12 resonated with you, this is a good starting point for gender-informed assessment and support.

Telehealth assessment: The expansion of telehealth since the pandemic has significantly widened access. Several Australian clinicians now offer AuDHD assessment entirely via video call, which removes the sensory and executive function barriers of travelling to an unfamiliar clinic and sitting in a waiting room whose lighting was apparently designed to simulate interrogation. Ask your GP for a referral to a telehealth-capable diagnostician, or search the directories above with a telehealth filter.

Medicare and costs: Diagnostic assessment for AuDHD in Australia typically costs between AUD 1,500 and AUD 3,500 out of pocket, depending on the clinician and the comprehensiveness of the assessment. Medicare rebates cover a portion of the cost if you have a Mental Health Treatment Plan from your GP, but the gap payment remains substantial. If cost is a barrier, university psychology clinics sometimes offer reduced-rate assessments supervised by registered psychologists. The wait is longer. The assessment is no less valid.

INTERNATIONAL

If you are outside Australia, the assessment landscape varies enormously by country. The UK's NHS pathway for adult AuDHD assessment currently involves waiting times measured in years rather than months, which is a level of institutional delay that would be considered a scandal in any other area of medicine and is considered normal in neurodevelopmental services. Private assessment is faster but expensive. In the US, insurance coverage for adult AuDHD assessment is inconsistent and often inadequate. In most of

Southeast Asia, adult AuDHD assessment is functionally unavailable outside major international hospitals in capital cities.

Wherever you are, the questions from Chapter 10 apply: does this clinician understand AuDHD as a co-occurring presentation? Do they work from a deficit model or an affirming one? Are they comfortable with an informed client? If the answer to any of these is no, keep looking.

Appendix B. Accommodation templates and advocacy tools

The accommodations described throughout this book are only useful if you can communicate them to the people and institutions that need to provide them. This appendix offers templates. Adapt them to your circumstances, your language, and your particular brand of neurodivergent needs. No template survives contact with a real bureaucracy unmodified, but having one is better than starting from a blank page when your executive function is already at capacity, which it will be, because the situations that require accommodation requests are the same situations that deplete the cognitive resources needed to write them.

WORKPLACE ACCOMMODATION REQUEST

A written accommodation request should include four elements. Your diagnosis, stated briefly and without apology. The specific functional limitations relevant to the workplace, not your entire diagnostic history but the aspects that affect your work. The specific accommodations you are requesting, with enough detail that someone who has never met a neurodivergent person could implement them. And the legal basis for the request, which in Australia is the Disability Discrimination Act 1992 and in most other jurisdictions is the equivalent legislation. Keep the tone professional and direct. You are providing information, not making a case for your worthiness. The accommodation is a legal right, not a favour, and the language should reflect that even when the workplace culture suggests otherwise.

EDUCATIONAL ACCOMMODATION REQUEST

For educational settings, the request follows the same structure but should include documentation of how the AuDHD profile specifically affects academic performance and assessment. The spiky profile from Chapter 7 is particularly useful here: naming the discrepancy between your strongest and weakest domains gives the institution a concrete reason for flexible assessment rather than a vague request for 'extra support.' Request specific accommodations: extra time, separate exam rooms, written instructions, permission for noise-cancelling headphones, flexibility in attendance requirements. The more specific you are, the harder it is for the institution to respond with the well-meaning but useless offer of 'general support.'

HEALTHCARE COMMUNICATION TEMPLATE

Chapter 10's advocacy toolkit described the process. The template: your name, your AuDHD diagnosis (with date and diagnosing clinician if available), a ranked list of your current concerns, any relevant medication and dosage information, and the specific requests you are making of this appointment. Print two copies. Give one to the doctor. Keep one for your medical autobiography. If you are navigating healthcare across languages, prepare the template bilingually, as Chapter 10 described. The three failed consultations at FV Hospital that taught me this lesson do not need to be your three failed consultations.

Appendix C. Daily tools and quick reference guides

Technology recommendations date faster than milk in the Vietnamese sun. What follows is less a specific product list and more a set of principles for choosing tools that work with an AuDHD brain, along with categories of tools that were useful at the time of writing. By the time you read this, half of them will have been updated, a quarter will have been acquired by a company that will ruin them, and the remaining quarter will be exactly what you need. Such is the lifecycle of productivity software.

PRINCIPLES FOR CHOOSING TOOLS

The tool should reduce executive function load, not add to it. If the setup takes longer than twenty minutes, your ADHD brain will abandon it before it becomes useful. If the interface is cluttered, your autistic brain will reject it on sensory grounds. If it requires daily maintenance to remain functional, you will maintain it for approximately one week before the dopamine of novelty wears off and the tool joins the graveyard of abandoned productivity systems that every AuDHD person maintains as an unofficial collection.

The best AuDHD tools are the ones that work passively. Automatic calendar reminders. Apps that block distracting websites without requiring you to decide in the moment whether to block them. Timers that announce themselves rather than requiring you to remember to check them. Environmental design beats willpower, as Chapter 15 argued, and the digital environment is as designable as the physical one.

CATEGORIES THAT HELP

Time awareness: Visual timers (Time Timer or equivalent) that make the passage of time visible rather than abstract. Phone alarms for transitions, set with a five-minute warning before the actual transition, because the AuDHD brain needs the runway. Calendar apps that send notifications you cannot easily dismiss.

Task management: Simple over complex. A single-list app beats a multi-project management system for most AuDHD daily needs. The goal is externalisation, getting the tasks out of working memory and onto a surface you can see, not project architecture. If your task management system has more features than a commercial aircraft cockpit, it is working for the system's designers rather than for you.

Sensory regulation: Noise-cancelling headphones remain the single most cost-effective AuDHD accommodation available. Brown noise or pink noise generators for focus. Blue-light filtering on screens after sunset. F.lux or equivalent for automatic screen colour temperature adjustment. These are not luxuries. They are the digital equivalent of the environmental design Chapter 5 described.

Body doubling: Virtual co-working platforms (Focusmate, Flow Club, or equivalent) that pair you with a stranger who is also trying to work, which sounds absurd until you try it and discover that the mere presence of another human being on a screen produces enough social accountability to keep your ADHD brain on task. Chapter 4's body doubling research explains why this works. The platforms just make it available without requiring you to have a friend who is free at 10am on a Tuesday.

Appendix D. The double empathy problem

The double empathy problem, first articulated by Damian Milton in 2012, is one of the most important conceptual shifts in autism research in the past two decades. It is also one of the most consistently misrepresented, so this appendix exists to state it clearly and to explain why it matters for AuDHD people specifically.

THE OLD MODEL

The traditional clinical model of autism positioned social communication difficulty as a deficit located inside the autistic person. Autistic people, in this framing, lacked Theory of Mind, the ability to understand that other people have different thoughts, feelings, and perspectives from their own. The implication was unidirectional: autistic people fail to understand neurotypical people, and the therapeutic task is to train autistic people to better understand, predict, and accommodate neurotypical social expectations. This model dominated clinical practice for decades and still informs most social skills training programmes, which are, in this light, programmes designed to teach autistic people to perform neurotypicality more convincingly, which is masking with a curriculum.

THE SHIFT

Milton's insight was that the communication breakdown between autistic and neurotypical people is bidirectional. Neurotypical people are as poor at understanding autistic communication as autistic people are at understanding neurotypical communication. The difficulty is not a deficit in one party but a gap between two different communicative systems, neither of which is inherently superior. Research has since confirmed this: studies show that autistic people communicate effectively with other autistic people, and neurotypical people communicate effectively with other neurotypical people, and the breakdown occurs at the boundary between the two groups. The difficulty is relational, not individual.

WHY THIS MATTERS FOR AUDHD PEOPLE

For AuDHD people, the double empathy problem is compounded by the fact that we are navigating not two but three communicative systems simultaneously: autistic, ADHD, and neurotypical. The autistic system values precision, consistency, and explicit communication. The ADHD system produces impulsive, associative, and often tangential communication. The neurotypical system that most social and professional environments operate in values neither autistic precision nor ADHD spontaneity but a particular kind of socially calibrated performance that requires reading implicit cues and producing contextually appropriate responses in real time.

The AuDHD person is translating between all three, continuously, and the translation cost is part of the masking burden this book has documented across fourteen chapters. Understanding the double empathy problem does not eliminate the cost. It does eliminate the assumption that the cost is your fault, which is a different kind of relief but a real one.

Key reference: Milton, D. E. M. (2012). On the ontological status of autism: The 'double empathy problem.' *Disability & Society, 27*(6), 883–887. https://doi.org/10.1080/09687599.2012.710008

Appendix E. Future horizons

Research moves faster than books. This appendix maps the research frontiers that are most likely to change the AuDHD landscape in the next five to ten years. Some of these are established programmes with funding and institutional momentum. Others are early-stage findings that may not replicate. All of them are worth watching, because the questions they are asking are the right questions, even if the answers are not yet settled.

GENETIC AND MOLECULAR MECHANISMS

The Homer1 gene research published in *Nature Neuroscience* in late 2025 (Rajasethupathy et al., 2025) suggests that attention may improve by reducing neural noise rather than by increasing stimulation, which challenges the pharmacological model that has dominated ADHD treatment for decades. If attention is a noise-reduction problem rather than a stimulation problem, the implications for medication design, non-pharmacological interventions, and our understanding of how ADHD and autism interact at the molecular level are substantial. This is early-stage research. It is also the kind of finding that changes the shape of the field when it replicates.

THE DEMENTIA AND NEURODEGENERATION CONNECTION

Chapter 3 and Chapter 13 documented the emerging evidence linking AuDHD to elevated dementia risk. This is the research frontier with the most immediate personal stakes for AuDHD adults currently aging. The key open questions: does the combined AuDHD profile carry a distinct dementia risk trajectory that differs from either condition alone? Is the risk primarily neurobiological (shared dopaminergic pathways, iron accumulation, neuroinflammation), primarily environmental (accumulated allostatic load from decades of mismatch), or an interaction of both? Does stimulant medication reduce risk, and if so, through what mechanism? The answers will require longitudinal studies of AuDHD adults specifically, which do not yet exist and should be a research priority.

IMMUNOLOGICAL CONNECTIONS

The MCAS and hypermobility (hEDS) connection documented in Chapter 6 via Weinstock et al. (2025) is part of a broader emerging picture of immune-neuropsychiatric interactions in neurodivergent populations. The finding that psychiatric symptoms improved after antihistamine treatment in MCAS patients raises the possibility that some of what we classify as neuropsychiatric conditions may have immunological components that current treatment protocols miss entirely. This is speculative but mechanistically plausible, and the clinical implications, if confirmed, would be significant: a subset of AuDHD adults experiencing anxiety, mood instability, and cognitive difficulties may benefit from immunological investigation and treatment rather than, or in addition to, psychotropic medication.

EPIGENETIC AGING AND ALLOSTATIC LOAD

Ciciurkaite et al. (2026) and related research on epigenetic aging clocks suggest that chronic psychosocial stress accelerates biological aging at the cellular level. For AuDHD adults, whose daily environmental mismatch produces chronic stress by design, the epigenetic aging pathway offers a measurable mechanism connecting lived experience to biological outcome. Future research tracking epigenetic age acceleration in neurodivergent populations, correlated with environmental factors and accommodation levels, could provide the evidence base for arguing that environmental accommodation is a health intervention with measurable biomarkers, not merely a quality-of-life improvement.

INCLUSIVE RESEARCH METHODOLOGIES

The A3ReAcH framework (Attitudes, Access, Awareness, Representation, Accommodation, and Health equity) represents a shift in how research about neurodivergent people is designed and conducted. The framework's existence is an acknowledgement that standard research methodologies have been excluding neurodivergent participants by design, producing an evidence base built disproportionately on neurotypical populations. Future research designed within inclusive frameworks will, over time, correct the biases documented in Chapter 10's discussion of clinical guidelines developed from unrepresentative samples.

AI IN ASSESSMENT AND CLINICAL PRACTICE

I explored this at length in *The Augmented Psychologist*. AI-assisted diagnostic tools, natural language processing for early detection, and machine learning models trained on neurodivergent communication patterns represent a genuine frontier for reducing diagnostic delay. The promise is real: an AI trained on a large enough dataset of

AuDHD presentations could, in principle, flag the pattern years before a human clinician notices it, particularly for the women and girls whose presentation Chapter 12 documented as systematically missed.

The risks are equally real: algorithmic bias reproducing the same diagnostic disparities in digital form, training data that underrepresents the populations most in need of identification, and the temptation to treat AI detection as diagnosis rather than as a screening tool that initiates a human clinical process. The technology is coming regardless. The question is whether it arrives with the biases of the system it is meant to improve, or whether someone builds it better. I am cautiously optimistic, which for a sixty-seven-year-old psychologist who has watched the field promise transformative technology approximately once per decade, is as enthusiastic as I get.

Appendix F. The Substack neurodiversity reading list

Chapter 11 described the Substack neurodiversity ecosystem in detail: why the platform works for neurodivergent readers, who the key voices are, and what the ecosystem's limitations are. This appendix is the practical version: a curated reading list organised by contribution type, with URLs and brief descriptions. All of these publications offer free content. Most also offer paid subscriptions that support the writers directly, which matters because every writer listed here is producing work that institutional research has not, and their ability to continue depends on readers who value what they produce.

This list was current at the time of writing. Substack publications launch, evolve, and occasionally go quiet. If a link has broken by the time you read this, search for the author by name on Substack. The work tends to persist even when the URL changes.

INFRASTRUCTURE AND SYSTEMIC ANALYSIS

Bridgette Hamstead – bridgettehamstead.substack.com – Founding Director of Fish in a Tree: Center for Neurodiversity

Education, Advocacy, and Activism. Neurodiversity Justice framework. Daily scholarship on AuDHD, late diagnosis, epistemic justice, dementia risk, and perimenopause. The ecosystem's most prolific and institutionally ambitious voice. Start here if you want the structural analysis.

Autistic Standpoint Theory – ishasnow on Substack – Sociological analysis of neurodivergent experience. Masking as political economy ('Frozen Capital'). Why psychology cannot see what sociology already knows. The theoretical backbone for systemic arguments about neurodivergence. Start here if Chapter 14 resonated.

PRACTICAL TOOLS AND SOCIAL ARCHITECTURE

Lindsey Mack, The Complexity Edge – thecomplexityedge.-substack.com – Practical architecture for rebuilding social life after unmasking. Taxonomy of post-unmasking positions. Step-by-step practices for connection. Start here if Chapter 9 left you wanting the instruction manual.

ACADEMIC TRANSLATION

Dr Gemma Williams, Neurodiverse Universe – neurodiverseuniverse.substack.com – Autistic academic researcher. Fortnightly newsletters and 'Beyond the Abstract' podcast episodes breaking down one research paper per instalment. Start here if you want to understand the research without drowning in it.

CLINICAL PRACTICE AND NEUROSCIENCE

Megan Anna Neff, Neurodivergent Notes – neurodivergentinsights.substack.com – Psychologist writing from the intersection of clinical practice and lived AuDHD experience. What neurodivergent-affirming clinical work actually looks like. Start here if you are navigating the therapy system.

Ana, Neuroscience and Psychotherapy – neuroscienceandpsy.substack.com – Neuroscience meets clinical practice. Interoception, body states, and mental health. Start here if Chapter 5's sensory material and Chapter 3's allostatic load argument left you wanting the brain science underneath.

Barbara (Blaze) Lazarony, Love on the Autism Spectrum – blazelazarony.substack.com – Licensed therapist. Neurodivergent relationships, nervous system dynamics, Pain Awareness Zones framework. Start here if Chapter 9's relationship material is where you live.

Based Psychiatrist – basedpsychiatrist.substack.com – Psychiatry examined from within. Newly launched and worth watching for the medicalisation angle.

LIVED EXPERIENCE AND ADVOCACY

Lyric Rivera, NeuroDivergent Rebel – neurodivergentrebel.substack.com – Trans autistic/ADHD educator and bestselling author. Radical self-acceptance. Collaborating with rather than battling against your neurodivergent mind. Start here if the deficit framing has exhausted you.

Jan De Kesel, Thinking-time – jandekesel.substack.com – AuDHD and anger as neurological response. Emotional intensity reframed. Start here if Chapter 6's emotional regulation discussion landed.

PART OF THE CONVERSATION

Lee Hopkins, Quiet Half – quiethalf.substack.com – This book's author. Clinical psychology, lived AuDHD experience, gentle contrarianism, expatriate life in the Vietnamese highlands, and the ongoing project of understanding a brain that took sixty-six years to be identified. I include myself here because pretending to observe the ecosystem from outside it would be less honest than admitting I live in it.

Subscribe to two or three that speak to where you are right now. Read what arrives. Don't try to keep up with everything, because the ADHD brain will want to subscribe to all of them immediately and the autistic brain will want to read everything in chronological order, and neither impulse will serve you. Let the rest arrive in its own time. The inbox will wait.

Griffin, S. (n.d.). *Sher the Cognitive Ecologist* [Substack newsletter]. Substack. https://shergriffin.substack.com

Hamstead, B. (n.d.). *NeuroJustice* [Substack newsletter]. Substack. https://bridgettehamstead.substack.com

Lazarony, B. (n.d.). *Love on the Autism Spectrum* [Substack newsletter]. Substack. https://blazelazarony.substack.com

Mack, L. (n.d.). *Lindsey Mack's Substack* [Substack newsletter]. Substack. https://lindseymackereth.substack.com

Mack, L. (n.d.). *The Complexity Edge* [Substack newsletter]. Substack. https://thecomplexityedge.substack.com

NeuroDivergent Rebel. (n.d.). *NeuroDivergent Rebel's Substack* [Substack newsletter]. Substack. https://neurodivergentrebel.substack.com

Snow, I. (n.d.). *Autistic Standpoint Theory* [Substack newsletter]. Substack. https://ishasnow.substack.com

About the Author

Lee Hopkins spent the first sixty-six years of his life being treated for the wrong condition. The diagnosis was Bipolar II. The reality, discovered in January 2025 after decades of medication, therapy, and increasingly creative forms of falling apart, was AuDHD—autism and ADHD, running in parallel, explaining everything and excusing nothing. AuDHD makes him a limited edition collector's item, apparently.

He is a counselling psychologist, organisational researcher, and writer. He holds a BSc (Hons) in applied psychology and sociology and a master's degree in counselling practice. His research on psychological contracts in organisations has been cited more than 450 times over the past 25 years, which tells you something about how workplaces quietly betray the people who trust them and, separately, that academics will cite almost anything if it confirms what they already suspected.

The fact that it is still being cited is proof of something, but he is not sure what. He knows it is enough to show he is smart, and also enough to show he knows nothing.

He served in the Royal Australian Air Force. He moved to England to be a rock star, failed miserably and ended up with an Honours degree, as you do. He spent a decade as one of Australia's early social media evangelists before burning out when the medium turned from a tool for human connection into a surveillance economy with better graphic design.

He has survived multiple business failures, long stretches of poverty, days without food, and bureaucratic systems that appear to have been purpose-built as endurance tests for people already running on empty.

He treats veterans experiencing depression, bipolar disorder, and trauma while quietly managing his own. His depression eventually lifted, not through better therapy or more medication, but because he moved to Đà Lạt, Vietnam. Same pension. Same brain. Different environment. Everything changed. The experience raised the question at the centre of his book, *It's the circumstances*: if the problem was always inside him, why did changing the outside fix it?

His photography has evolved from monochromatic, melancholic, moody landscapes to vibrant colour, which he considers the most persuasive evidence he has that environments shape perception more than most psychology textbooks are willing to admit. For decades he wrote music that friends kindly described as 'music to slash your wrists by'. These days he writes funk-metal, which is probably diagnostic of something.

A client and friend of his, David Boloker, retired CTO at IBM, wrote this about him:

> *Equal parts adventurer and truth-teller, Lee blends psychological insight with lived experience. He's incisive without being clinical, funny without being slick, and relentlessly humane. He has that infectious optimism that all adventurers need, despite whatever shit they find themselves in.*

He lives in Đà Lạt with a view of pine forests, a daily dinner routine with his wife Hương, and the cautious optimism of someone who has learned that recovery sometimes arrives with the production values of regional community television: underfunded, slightly awkward, and available only to those who know where to find the channel.

This is not his first book. He has learned not to predict whether it will be his last.

Lee online

You can find Lee at:

- quiethalf.com
- mindblownpsychology.com
- leehopkinsphotography.com
- youtube.com/@LeeHopkins
- leehopkins.com
- leehopkinswriter.com

Also by Lee Hopkins

- **The Convenient Monster:** Best read if you suspect some social problems survive because the story we tell about them is more comforting than the truth
- **Harder than it should be:** After COVID we did not return to normal. We adjusted to chronic strain and called it resilience
- **Misdiagnosed:** When psychiatry mistakes neurodivergence for mental illness
- **It's the circumstances:** A psychologist's contrarian guide to depression, systems, and why your brain might be fine
- **You're not imagining it, it IS this weird:** Notes on surviving the optimisation trap
- **Understanding AuDHD:** A comprehensive guide (3rd edition)
- **Embracing neurodiversity:** Understanding and thriving with your unique brain
- **Living with Bipolar II:** Understanding, managing, thriving
- **The Augmented Psychologist:** How to stay human, stay useful, and stay sane in the age of AI

www.ingramcontent.com/pod-product-compliance
Lightning Source LLC
LaVergne TN
LVHW100310210926
848480LV00003B/1077